Give Them
Roots, Wings
and Bonds for Life

An intentional family's love story

Gustavo León Zenteno

VITALITY
buzz, bliss + books

Give Them Roots, Wings and Bonds for Life:
An Intentional Family's Love Story
Copyright © 2025 by Gustavo León Zenteno
Published by VITALITY buzz, bliss + books LLC
vitalitybuzz.org

ISBN: 978-1-954688-36-0

In gratitude

**to the VATRONS
who breathed life into my book
by sponsoring the publication**

Víctor Aguilar, Diana Angélica López, Héctor Ariza, Rubén Ávila, Leah Beltz, Francisco Cadena, Catalina Campos, Javier Cano, Beatriz Cárdenas, Mario Chávez, Fran Cherny, Mark Christenson, Stephanie Colores, José María Contreras, Morgan Donegan, Jim Eutsler, Luis Fuentes, Mauricio Gallegos, Patricia Gallegos Macías, Lydia García, Myrna Gómez, Abel Gómez González, Anaís Graterol, Santiago Gutiérrez, Natalia Hollander, Mónica Jerez, Stacey Kinser, Hugo León Sr. & Beatriz Zenteno, Hugo León Zenteno, Beatriz León Zenteno, Luis Arturo León Zenteno, Verónica León Sandoval, Andrea León-Ramos, Fernando León-Ramos, Rodrigo León-Ramos, Isabel Méndez, Juan Andrés Mercado, Molly Montgomery, Karen Anne Oconnell, Verónica Pando, Mario Pérez, César Ramos Sr. & María Elena Rico, César Ramos Rico, Claudia Ramos Rico, Fernando Ramos Rico, Raúl Ramos Rico, Sergio Ramos Rico, Miguel Ángel Ruiz Torres, Rick Scheeler, Tobias Schmitz, Ann Schulte, Phiroza Setna, Brian Shircliff, María Soler, Salvador Soto, Carlos Suárez, Lucía Suárez, Sergio Talavera, Ángel Tramontín, María José Vega, Antonio Villagómez, Aldo Vivó, Bryan Wright

A very special thank you to Rodrigo León-Ramos for the design of the artwork for the front and back covers, to Héctor Ariza for his ideas on the layout of the front cover, and to Julie Lucas for bringing them to life into the book.

Dedication

To Marisela, Andrea, Fernando and Rodrigo;
Thank you for filling my life with love
and inspiring me every day
to give you my best, forever.

To my parents, Beatriz and Hugo,
and my wife's parents, María Elena and César;
Thank you for being our role models
of Roots, Wings and Bonds
for the entire family and specially for Marisela and me.

To our siblings and their own families;
Thank you for accompanying us, from near and far,
and always being there, through our crazy journey.

To all families, in any configuration,
that already live their own rituals and traditions;
I wish they continue nurturing them and
renewing their love and dedication every day.

To all new couples that, with love, faith and hope,
decide to embark upon the wonderful adventure
of becoming parents,
I toast to them, so they are always intentional!

CONTENTS

Introduction
9

Roots

Wings

Bonds

Introduction

I wrote this book for the grandchildren of our grandchildren, hoping our family will continue and thinking that one day, when they look back and the little kids ask their parents, "where do we come from?" and "why do we do our traditions and rituals?" they can talk about what is in this book and realize we have shared values that have grown stronger and evolved with time through generations within our family.

I also wrote this book for other parents, and other families, hoping to inspire the desire and intentionality to live a happy and fulfilling family life. I don't pretend to say that our story is in any way a model or reference. Like any family, we've had our share of ups and downs, problems and adversity as well as wonderful moments of happiness. What you will see in this book is a selection of stories of the things we cherish the most, many of them have significant learning for us as a family and a reflection of things we want to continue doing moving forward. My wish is that anyone reading this book can relate to some of the stories and identify something that they do with their families or would like to try in their own way, within their own particular context. My sole intention is to share our life story and hopefully others will see some value for their own journey.

I am a big fan of life quotes. I believe quotes are sparks of wisdom that make you stop, think and inspire you to grow as a person. There is one quote that did just that for me regarding the way we've decided to raise our family, it is by the Dalai Lama and says:

**"Give the ones you love
wings to fly, roots to come back to and reasons to stay."**

In such a simple phrase you have a lifetime philosophy for a family to live by. The first part is pretty clear, to "**give them wings to fly**" is every parent's aspiration, to prepare your kids to go out into the world and be able to not only care for themselves but to thrive, to go places, travel, experience and enjoy life and to always grow and flourish. That is what "give them wings to fly" means to me.

The second part "**give them roots to come back to**" is also simple. As parents, we want our kids to remember where they come from, where they developed and grew as individuals and as a family, to connect with their extended family, to learn about their past, and honor their shared history. A solid foundation, a root that supports our family, a place they call home and come back to whenever they want, whenever they need, those roots nurture your soul, are a safe haven where they can recharge; it is where they reconnect with their values and reunite with the rest of the family. They re-energize to go out again and fly into the world. That is what "give them roots to come back to" means to me.

The last part "and reasons to stay" is the one I see a little differently. I see it as giving them a strong sense of belonging with **lifetime bonds to keep the entire family connected**, so as the kids grow up they would want to be together and bring their families together, no matter how old they are or where they are. A family is for life, it is not just a phase in your life; we all can enjoy expressing our continuous love and interaction and provide that sense of belonging to every new member for life. It goes beyond reasons to stay which sounds more oriented to a family visit.

More than reasons to stay, we want to have such strong bonds that keep our family together through space and time. They feel the need to share their experiences and continue being an important part of their lives, no matter where they are located. They look after each other and constantly provide support when they need it. They share their hopes and dreams and continue growing together along the journey. Therefore, I decided on the title as:

"Give Them Roots, Wings and Bonds for Life"

As I have been remembering all the stories for this book, it has been a source of joy and gratitude writing each chapter; I get a boost of endorphins with the memories, and a boost of dopamine once I finished writing the chapter. I also discovered that both my wife and I brought our own set of rituals and traditions from our own families before we married. Things like dancing, how my father taught me to dance since I was very little, and now it is something that I passed on to our three kids. Others, like regularly traveling with parents, even after getting married, it is something that my wife's father leads as frequently as possible and they have done for years and still do to this day, and we do now with our adult kids as well. Other things like preserving meaningful keepsakes and pictures from all the important milestones and also from the seemingly mundane experiences of our kids' lives is something that I learned from watching my mother do it. The habit of having regular "cafecitos" (coffee dates) with each one of our kids is something that my wife learned from her mom as well. The way my father tickled me and my siblings with his "tiki-tiki" walking fingers on the table and his "araña magaña" hand gesture (magaña spider) to make us laugh so hard and squirm all over and how I do the same things with my kids. The very early walks to "el bosque de Tlalpan" (a nearby forest in Mexico City) with my wife's mother and her father to see squirrels and get an orange juice afterwards is also something we have done and still do with our kids whenever we can.

These are just some examples of rituals that we brought into our combined family life. The beauty of these rituals is that they have been part of our lives during our formative years so there is no need to explain or learn why they are important or how to do them, we just know by having lived them. This made the adoption simple and enjoyable.

This realization is very important and something that cannot be taken for granted. The idea of cherishing rituals and traditions learned from our parents and passing them down to the next generation is at the core of our humanity. It is that willingness to preserve and transfer what makes a family special, and by having more and more families being intentional doing similar things, it weaves the tapestry of our beautiful cultures around the world. Like Mother Teresa said, "If you want to change the world, go home and love your family", I believe that is how we make a difference in our society, one family at a time.

This is now more important than ever, when the family concept has evolved to cope with the demands of our modern life. The constellation of different types of families is very different today from what it was decades or centuries ago. The evolution of technology, where social media, screen time, convenience and comfort, and the faster pace of life, have improved overall access to things; and ubiquitous information and artificial intelligence have enhanced human capability to do more, and it pulls harder and harder towards individualism and human isolation. The paradox is that with all these fantastic capabilities, we believe that we are connected by virtue of having 24/7 digital social media and that we can be far more efficient in our time and what we do, but in reality, we are more and more disconnected from meaningful human connection.

The central idea of this book is about a family being deliberate, thoughtful and proactive about how to make the most of our time together and choosing to be present in our lives vs. being reactive to the circumstances and being pulled into so many different directions that distract us from what is truly important in life: to establish common roots, to prepare our kids to fly, and to accompany them along the way for the rest of our lives.

In the same way we put that level of intentionality into our work lives, where leaders, managers and employees are intentional about defining visions, purpose and goals for their companies, organizing teams, defining structures and finding ways to make meaningful connections, figuring out ways to solve complex problems while taking care of each employee in the process, I strongly believe we need the same level of intentionality in our family life. Ultimately, a family is the most important enterprise of all, the most relevant team we could be a part of, with aspirations and dreams for each member and with a clear purpose to achieve in life. Why not dedicate our best efforts to raising our game in our family life with the people that we care most about?

For that matter, in this book I have woven ideas, concepts and some practical tips on family life that are connected to my learnings as a human resources leader working with organizations, teams, leaders and managers at all levels for more than 30 years.

As I say this, I would like to clarify that I am no expert studying family life. My experience is what I have lived with my family and that is what I am sharing in this book. There are other wonderful resources for in-depth learning that I recommend for elevating your understanding and preparation to lead your family life. Like anything that matters, we master what we dedicate our time and attention to. Here are some outstanding resources to continue learning from true experts in this field:

The Intentional Family –
Simple Rituals to Strengthen Family Ties
William J. Doherty, Ph.D.

The 7 Habits of Highly Effective Families –
Creating a Nurturing Family in a Turbulent World –
Stephen R. Covey

Like many movies or books say at the beginning, "based on a true story", that is in fact the case of this book. There is no fiction. All the stories are real, with real characters, and have the added bonus of integrating my thoughts as I view them in retrospect. This book is about the family journey that Marisela and I started more than 31 years ago that has become a wonderful marriage with three fantastic young adults in Andrea, Fernando and Rodrigo. It is a recollection of lessons learned, reflections along the way and many simple things we still do a few decades later.

I love music and I believe it is an incomparable form of communication as it sparks emotion and evokes precious memories. Music can take you places you have been, remember people you were with, and relive the moment like you are there again. Many times, I will be listening to a song, and I will think of a moment or experience lived as a family. Music is so important in our family life that in each story I added suggested songs to listen to as I believe they relate to the topic and can help to round up the experience of reading this book. My invitation is that as you finish reading each story, play the recommended songs and read the lyrics. I hope this brings you joy and if you like it, you can consider adding it to your playlists. At the end of the book, I assembled a music playlist for the book that you can access on Spotify using this QR code:

On every story I also volunteered a few specific "key takeaways" to summarize the insights from the things I learned with our own family. You can consider these as suggestions and main tips that, if anything, can serve as food for your own thoughts as you plan how to live your family life to the fullest.

I see this as our "family book" reflecting some of our own story so far. The journey is still in progress, so new chapters will be added in future editions for sure but those are yet to be lived first…

Roots

*"Families are like branches on a tree,
we grow in different directions,
yet our roots remain one."*

To talk about roots is to talk about those stories that formed the essence of our family, since we started as a couple and how we nurtured those early years with meaningful activities and invested our time creating special core memories that molded the shape of each family member to become who we are today.

In the first two chapters I talk about me, which is not usually what I do when I interact with others. I am not used to being the center of attention (unless I am dancing!) but I believe it is important to share my first learning, which is the need to invest in oneself in order to be able to give our best to others. This is something that I experienced in my profession as a human resources leader, working with all kinds of leaders and managers and their teams, and it boils down to a very simple concept: "You cannot give what you don't have".

If you are not clear on your purpose, goals, and aspirations, it will be more difficult to help others find their purpose or feel inspired. If you are out of balance in your work and personal life, it will be harder to teach balance to your loved ones. If you are not handling conflicts well it will be more difficult to help your kids learn healthy behaviors in their interactions with others. I believe that parents need to constantly invest in themselves, to get clarity on their own path, individually and as a couple, to regularly seek care and enjoyment for themselves, so they can be at their best for their families.

It also reminded me that so much of family life is taught on the spot, learning by doing, and setting the example of anything we would like our family to do. This requires being present and dedication when it matters most. I believe that more than half of whatever achievements we aspire to attain in any of the roles that we choose in life come from just showing up and not giving up. So, in my view, to increase the chances of showing up, I need to invest in myself, in my own care, on being clear on what I want to do in life, and where I consciously choose not to engage so I have the energy that I need to fully engage with my family and never give up. This is why the first two chapters are about me.

Then I talk about my wife and I as a couple, our vows and the key learnings of a few things we have done that have marked the essence of our family. This is where the foundation of strong roots starts. Like concentric circles that start with yourself, your own roots as an individual, finding your sense of purpose, values, principles, goals and then expand to your spouse/life partner, to learn about their own roots as an individual, their sense of purpose, values, principles, goals and aspirations. From there, we formed our combined roots and started growing our family together.

Song:

"Hasta la Raíz" – Natalia Lafourcade

Every MVP Needs a PVP

"Vision without action is a daydream,
Action without vision is a nightmare." – Japanese Proverb

In sports, at the end of a long, highly competitive tournament, when the championship game is over, usually there is a trophy for the MVP, the Most Valuable Player. This coveted award goes to that player who was the ultimate role model, the one who pulled the team forward to win. When they receive the award and get interviewed, they describe how they dreamed with that moment, how they visualized themselves winning the championship and receiving this award. This vision became the fuel for their daily sacrifice in training, in many cases for years and after several previous attempts to win without success. Then, they describe how after being so close to winning and being devastated by the loss, they looked at their vision and got back to training harder, every day until they had another opportunity for the championship and ultimately, they succeeded.

A similar "MVP effect" happens in many types of awards. Be it the Academy Awards (Oscars), the Nobel Prize, the Pulitzer Prize, the Grammys, etc. In all these events, the acceptance speech has in many cases the same elements around how the recipient had a high sense of purpose, a mission to dedicate their life to, a clear vision of them fulfilling that purpose, accepting the award, and doing it on their own terms, living by their own set of principles.

Can we get the same level of drive, clarity of vision, and determination to pursue in our personal lives and with our families? Is there an MVP award for a father, mother, sibling, employee, friend? I think there is. While the recognition may not always be public, or it does not happen in one event, I can say you get it in multiple moments through life. You get it when you accomplish cherished milestones in your marriage, when you have a child, when you celebrate what your members of the family accomplish. When I turned 50 years young, I got my MVP award as a father. It was awarded unexpectedly by my 3 kids when each of them gave a toast speech at my birthday party. Their speeches had everything I wish one day they would say about me. And I realized that after so many "seasons" playing the role of a father, my wife and kids had given me the "Father MVP Award". It was so emotional, so genuine and heartfelt, so sweet that no other award can compare.

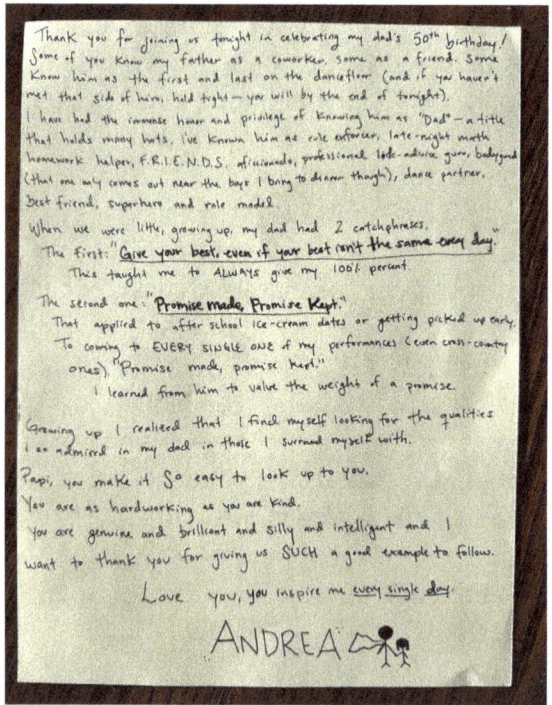

Papá,
I think it is fair to say that
everyone has someone they admire
and look up to in life. I want to thank
you for being that person for me.
For each of the past 18 years, I have
attempted to be more and more like
you. Your morals, values, goals for yourself,
and for the 5 of us are things that
I hope, I can too possess one day in
my life. You've truly been the example of
what makes a great father, passions
we share for things such as sports, movies,
friends and much more however, have made
you more than just a dad to me. To me,
you've truly been my best friend throughout
life. Whether it's playing football or suffering
through golf in 110° weather, I always have
a great time when I am with you. You've
never failed to be by my side, so for that,
I thank you; and for countless other things
I am so grateful for. You've given us all
a better life than we could've ever
wished for, so thank you for that too.
I love you so much, and Happy Birthday.

—Guigo

This helped me realize that like those players that for years dreamed of their MVP moment, in our roles as parents, or spouses, brothers, sisters, we can also set goals and visualize ourselves having an MVP moment of joy with our families. To be clear, I am not advocating for the self-serving, ego-centered connotation that usually comes associated with the concept of having an award. I believe parents by nature are selfless and we give everything, including our lives, to our families without expecting anything in return. That is how we are wired by nature, as our reward is seeing the happiness and growth of our kids, that is all we need. I am using the comparison with an MVP award as a way to spark our intentionality of charting a course, of having a vision, moving beyond living and reacting to the day-to-day circumstances and events, with the sole intent of living a meaningful life and seeing all family members flourishing.

But where do you start? You start by defining for yourself what you want in life, what your purpose is, your vision and your goals. In my case, I started when I was in college, and I had the great opportunity to read Steven Covey's book **The 7 Habits of Highly Effective People**. The first habit is to **Be Proactive** which is all about taking conscious responsibility for your own life, to be self-aware and use your freedom to choose your response to any event or circumstance that you cannot control. It is all about focusing on the only thing you can control, which is your behavior, your actions. Then the second habit you learn is to **Begin with the End in Mind**. You start by picturing the last part of your life, when you are celebrating your 100th birthday and your loved ones are talking about your life, your legacy, and the impact you've had on them and others. It is called a life mission statement. I decided to write mine for the first time and called it my personal PVP: Purpose, Vision, Principles.

I wrote my first PVP early in my 20's, one day on my birthday. I printed it and put it in a place where I could see it every day and have been doing so ever since. I have it in my room, on a wall near where I dress up in the mornings. I started reading it every morning, investing 5 minutes visualizing how I could live that day by those words. I've been doing this for more than 35 years. Here I share snapshots of the most recent one, done for 2025:

My **PURPOSE** *in life*:

Be happy, love and grow the gifts I received from God and use them to serve others. Today the world is better because of my existence. I am a spark that enables individuals to discover their purpose, grow and flourish, to live happily with their families, and to lead their companies consciously and with love.

My **VISION** *of myself*:

I am a holistic and conscious human being; I enjoy each moment and live intensely every stage of my life. I am authentic and congruent with myself and with others. I believe that a sincere smile and kindness can open any door.

I am physically, mentally, emotionally and spiritually healthy. I take care and respect my body, mind and soul by feeding them only good & positive things. I enjoy both being active and recovering. I live a fulfilling and flourishing life.

I let my actions speak up for my beliefs and convictions; I focus my energy doing today the things I can control and can influence, in order to have a better tomorrow. I recognize the things I cannot control; I accept them with peace, and I leave them in God's hands to do the changes that are needed. I see adversities only as temporary and treat them as growth opportunities.

Every day I learn something important that helps me grow as a person. In each experience of my life, I either learn or teach something. I understand that everything happens in my life for a reason and contributes to fulfilling my purpose.

I use my talents, virtues, and capacity to serve others and stretch myself every day to grow so I can expand my impact on others. I influence my community so together we create a better world for our kids and raise our kids, encourage, and support them so they can make the world even better in the future.

I recognize that I need others to be happy and to enjoy the pleasure of loving and being loved. I am interdependent with others. I trust in the good and capability of others, knowing there is abundant love and wellness for all.

My **KEY ROLES** where I will engage to the fullest are:

SPIRITUAL   Nurture my relationship with God and grow my faith through practicing love and service to others.

SELF   Love myself. Accept me as I am. Exercise daily, eat and sleep well. Learn, create, give back.

HUSBAND   Choose to love, honor and give my best to Marisela every day. Be present, enjoy each moment. Have fun together!

FATHER   Love Andrea, Fernando & Rodrigo. Be present. Give them my best every day. Help them discover and pursue their passions, understand the

	purpose of their lives and succeed in whatever they choose to do so they live a happy and fulfilling life.
MY 3rd ACT	Love what I do. Show up and start before I am ready. I am a philanthropist, writer, coach, advisor, athlete, dancer, musician, traveler.
FAMILY	Love Parents & Siblings. Enjoy time spent together. Look after them and help them be happy.

The **PRINCIPLES** that guide my behaviors are:

Trust God	I know I have a special purpose for my life, and I live it faithfully. Everything happens for good.
Respect Natural Laws	If I want to harvest, I need to plant the seeds first. Everything has its own timing and process. I accept it and invest as necessary to maximize my capacity to influence desired outcomes.

Treat others as they would like to be treated

I put myself into others' shoes. I seek first to understand then to be understood. I do not judge. I always listen to understand how I can help. I look for both sides of the story all the time.

Be Present   I devote my undivided attention and bring my best and authentic self to every situation and relationship that really matters. I enjoy and experience the "here and now" to fully live every moment.

Be Transparent   I am the same everywhere. I always tell the truth. I openly share my feelings.

Make Things Happen   I take action and always keep my promises. I choose my attitude and my habits and focus my energy on my circles of control and influence. I act with passion, conviction, consistency and faith to reach my goals and fulfill my purpose.

Make Things Simple   I believe there is an easy, natural and logical way of doing things. I trust my intuition, emotions, and common sense.

Be Patient and Peaceful   With myself and with others. First reactions sometimes can really harm. I believe conflicts can be solved without fighting or damaging relationships.

Be Humble and Generous   I know how to give and receive. I believe small details and good manners make a big difference. A personal touch is always appreciated.

Over time I realized the key was to go beyond the concepts and to define a few specific and actionable Goals and the supporting Habits to bring them to life for that year. I chose to have just a few more specific goals for each one of the key roles in my life (spiritual, self, spouse, father, professional, extended family). Then I decided to review progress on my next birthday. I adjusted a few words on my PVP as my life changed, based on new experiences and new aspirations I wanted to accomplish. I think our life is organic, it changes, we adapt as we grow and our vision of ourselves evolves accordingly. And our goals change every year as well. Making this a living document, an ongoing process is what makes it relevant and what drives a sense of fulfillment. Having the habit of looking at it regularly, in the good and bad days, gives you clarity of purpose and direction for those times when you feel lost, it helps you remember and reconnect with yourself.

---

*My **GOALS** by Dec 2025 and supporting **HABITS**:*

Nurture my soul – Music, Dance; Nightly: Gratitude, Pray, Meditate; Daily 1% better (30 min each): Piano, Read-Write, Learn Italian.

Be more social – Seek friends (1 - 2 per week), do something fun frequently (Tennis, Golf, Bowling, Nature, Collaborate, Just hang-out).

Be sustainably fit – Sleep 10:00 pm; Exercise 1 hr daily, (Strength, Walk-Run, Sprint). Eat well (Veggies first, No sugar, Healthy choices).

Be a fun date! – Enjoy Cincinnati and California. Live new experiences, do things we like: travel, dinner, dance, movies, sports, friends.

Be present - Andrea: Launch Miss Andy, support her plans for day-job enrichment; Kris-get closer; Fernando: Prepare wedding, Jaxon-get closer, meet his family; Rodrigo: **Atomic Habits**, Social network, and how to support his plans for 2026.

Be proactive – 524ever biz plan & partnerships; Coaching CB Cert; Tax strategy/Investments; Home refinance; Medical check (Sept).

Travel: Florida (Feb); Mexico (Apr, Dec); Road Trip (June); Sta Clarita (June, Nov-Dec); 524 trip to Japan-Korea (Sept).

I also realized this can be a very meaningful way to share with others, those closest to you, a view of who you are and who you want to become. I shared it with my wife as a way for her to get to know me better and to share my goals, aspirations, and dreams. I've also taken the risk of sharing with some close friends and some of my close colleagues and even a few of my bosses and senior leaders at work. The result has always been positive, it sparks a dialogue, I get questions on some of the concepts, and I've gotten great insights and feedback that I've incorporated into the document over the years.

Seeing how impactful this has been in my life, I thought I could teach our kids to get started doing this, to begin finding their purpose and creating their own goals in a very simple way. So, we started a family tradition, every new year, to do our personal visualization of aspirations and goals to achieve in a year.

We started when they were just a few years old with a simple concept, with a blank sheet of paper and a few magazines. We asked each family member to select around 5 important images of things they saw themselves accomplishing in the new year. It could be anything, a resolution, a personal goal, just a hobby or a thing they really wanted to do or see themselves becoming. We facilitated the means by bringing magazines, scissors and glue sticks and taught them how to make a collage by sticking them together in one sheet of paper, putting the year and their name at the top. Then we asked each family member to share with the rest what they chose and why this was important to them. Then each one posts their own collage in their bedroom, in a place where they can see it every day. We mounted a personal "vision board" in each of their rooms. And each one of them chose to add other things to their board, many of them related to their goals and aspirations. In July of each year, I would give each family member a reminder by asking them how they were doing with their plans. Then on the following New Year's Day, we will do it again. We start with each family member sharing how they did vs. the last year's plans and repeat the tradition of setting new aspirations for the new year.

Over the years this became a very meaningful family tradition. I've kept an archive of each of their individual sheets from year to year and we can see how each kid has become a teenager and then an adult. They have learned to set goals, make choices and work towards their aspirations. Very importantly, we all share as a family, we all feel part of each other's goals and in many ways, we help each other to achieve them. We have seen them learn to adjust, adapt and in many cases, deal with failure for not achieving what they wanted and try again the following year, or move on to a new goal.

It all starts with sparking your purpose in your life, so you can infuse that energy into other family members. You cannot give others what you don't have. Once you have it, you can find a simple and fun way to engage your family in discovering their own.

Andrea (2007 & 2024)

Fernando (2007 & 2024)

Rodrigo (2007 & 2024)

Marisela (2007 & 2024)

Gustavo (2007 & 2024)

Key Takeaways:

We can have the same level of intentionality with our families as we do in our professional lives.

To be an MVP for your family, you can start by defining your own PVP (Purpose, Values, Principles).

Goals and Habits are the key to bringing your PVP to life in the key roles you want to fully engage.

Share your PVP with your family, make it a ritual, consider doing the activity of Vision Boards on New Years.

Tips to develop your own PVP:

Read Habit #2 from Stephen Covey's book – **The 7 Habits of Highly Effective People**

Think about these questions to get started:

- If your life was a movie, what would be the title? What would be the happy ending?

- If you were doing a billboard of your life, what would it say? What images would it have?

- What would a 30 second ad of your life say?

Songs:

"Man in the Mirror" – Michael Jackson

"Hacia Lo Alto" – Eduardo Ortiz

My Private Victory – My Place to Re-energize

"Today I shall behave as if this is the day
I will be remembered by." – Dr. Seuss

I believe in celebrating accomplishment, and more importantly, in the private victory it represents when we reach a goal, and the boost of energy and self-confidence to anyone's life that comes with that special moment. I think this is way more important than receiving whatever trophy or memento for doing something special.

Usually, recognition is short-lived and forgotten, and the trophies often end up being stored away, collecting dust, or even thrown into the trash, but the feeling of doing something great, reliving the moment and the emotion is something that you can experience forever. When we have moments of greatness in our lives, I wish we could find a way to "bottle that feeling" so we are able to relive those moments and get that boost of energy when we need it the most.

I think this is why many sports teams display their championship trophies near their locker rooms or training facilities, or why other teams that hang huge pennants with the years of their championships won at their stadiums, or why on the major tennis tournaments the names and pictures of the previous years' winners are largely displayed on the corridor from the dressing room to the court, or why companies proudly display their public recognition and rankings prizes at their office's reception lobbies and boardrooms. It is all about reminding whoever is playing the game the moments of greatness of that individual, team or institution.

At our home, there is one room that is entirely mine and I've converted it into my place to re-energize. It is "My Private Victory" room. Some people have their "man caves", others have their "she-sheds" or their gardens, garages full of tools, etc. I have a room where I display the things about which I feel most proud, and I also have a space to be creative and to stretch/exercise. This is where I regain my confidence, where I remind myself of all the things I can do, all that I have accomplished in the different areas of my life. This is the place where I focus on my own development and growth.

There is a very unique spark that connects my mind and my body when I work out and lift my eyes and see a milestone I achieved, or a recognition I received by others. It reminds me that if I want to achieve a goal, I need to put in daily effort, sweat and push myself out of my comfort zone, to go farther, knowing my limits, and take a moment to recover when needed. And then I get back at it the next morning, until finally there is a new reason to be proud of myself as there is a new accomplishment to be displayed in my room.

Recently I read a very popular book called **Atomic Habits** by James Clear. I think it is a wonderful guide on how to establish habits in your life in a consistent manner, with easy and practical concepts that anyone can apply. One of the things that most attracted my attention from the book is how relevant the environment can be where we are to nurture our habits and the importance of intentionally designing it to increase the chances of success.

Here is what James Clear says in his book about this: "Environment design is powerful not only because it influences how we engage with the world but also because we rarely do it. Most people live in a world others have created for them. But you can alter the spaces where you live and work to increase your exposure to positive cues and reduce your exposure to negative ones. Environment design allows you to take back control and become the architect of your life. Be the designer of your world and not merely the consumer of it."

Even before I read this, I had the intuition of having my private victory room designed by myself to help me put into practice the habits that connect with my purpose and goals and increase the chances of being consistent at it. Reading **Atomic Habits** I found validated my intuition to do this.

My room has all my books at arm's reach in bookshelves that I organized thematically according to how my brain is structured. As I decided to learn to play the piano, I put a small electric keyboard right next to my desk. I want to stay active during the day and move my body so I have a small trampoline where I can jump for a few minutes as I take breaks from sitting down. I also put a step-stride below my desk so I can pedal while I am sitting down for an extended period of time. And I have a space to put my yoga mat and stretch during the day as needed.

On a wall, I placed all the meaningful recognitions I received from people that have helped me grow as a person and of special teams and moments of interaction as wonderful memories of my journey. I purposely keep all these at home, not in any office I've worked. These are my private victory reminders.

I am a fan of the **Star Trek** television series, which is about humanity's desire to constantly evolve and grow to go out and meet new people, to explore and venture into the unknown. In all the **Star Trek** space ships, the captains have their "Ready Room" which is where they meet with their staff, where they receive important calls, retreat to think, study and plan ahead.

It is not called an office or studio or anything like that. This concept inspired me to call this my "Ready Room" and I put that sign on the door. This is my place, where every day I am ready to continue growing as a human being.

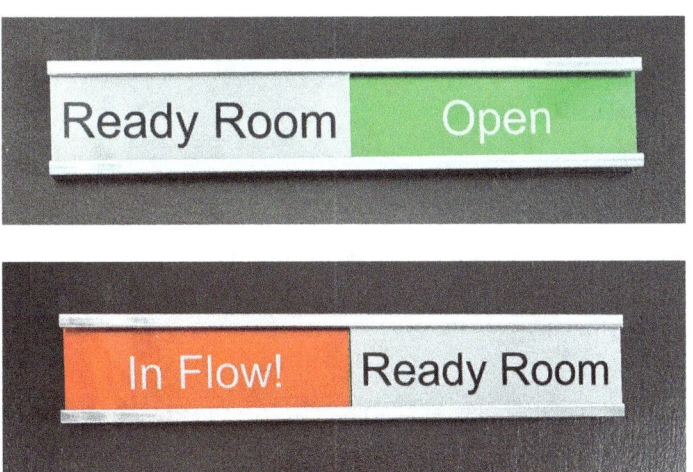

This works for me. I like structure, order and clear spaces with a purpose for each area whenever possible. I realize and value different approaches for other people, including my own family members, according to their own needs and personalities. I believe the execution of this idea can look very different, person by person. What I am advocating for is to have intentionality on what a person wants to do with their space, instead of just being reactive to it.

As an example, working from home as many people continue doing since the last pandemic, it certainly is different from a level of energy and inspiration to just wake up and right at your bed, take the video conference lying down, with the headphones and a laptop, without the camera on, than waking up earlier, exercising, showering, dressing comfortably, and going to a room or desk that is designed for you to work. And if you work at the office or have a blended/hybrid work arrangement, still when you get home, there are times when you work from there, or have personal projects or interests in mind. I believe that the environment where those endeavors are pursued will greatly influence the productivity, effectiveness and satisfaction while doing them.

Key Takeaways:

Visual motivation fuels inspiration.

Reminding yourself of your moments of greatness can bring you positive energy when you are down, when you need it the most.

Find your own space, your place to re-energize, to recharge and to be ready for the day, to be ready for your family, to be ready for the world.

Be intentional with the design of your space, no matter how small or big it may be. Make it yours.

Songs:

"This is My Time" – Amy Stroup

"Where My Heart Will Take Me" – Diane Warren, Russell Watson

Our Vows – Our Daily Choice

"Falling in love is not a choice.
To stay in love is." – John Spence

The most meaningful part of a wedding ceremony in all cultures, in any spiritual setting, is the exchange of vows. This is the moment when the couple declares their love, commitment and choice to give their life to each other. Given this is the true essence of the ritual, I wonder, why would anyone just read something generic, or something they did not think or write themselves? Or why would any couple just repeat what the minister or priest is telling them to say? My wish for anyone choosing to get married is that they write their own vows.

This is the moment you are choosing to get married so say it, from the bottom of your heart and with all your reason, say it clear, say it loud! The ceremony, the party, and anything around this moment are secondary. You chose to be together, for the rest of your lives, so it is your moment to say it, in your own words.

Being so important, so memorable and so emotional, I believe that moment of choice is not just for the wedding day. I believe that as a couple, each of us can make this choice every morning. While on your wedding day you choose to get married, every day you choose to stay married and bring those commitments to life; some days it is easy, everything flows, all works smoothly and is all about happiness and smiles, and some days, oh well, it just takes some extra effort.

For our marriage, we wrote our vows, then we printed them, signed them and posted them in our bedroom, in a place where we both can see them. Every morning, I have a personal ritual:

I wake up, I put my wedding ring on my finger, I look at our vows and say to myself "I choose to stay married, to honor Marisela, to love her and give her my best today". I read our vows and remember that moment when we made that choice for the first time. Then I kiss Marisela and go on to start my day. I do it every day, for the last 31 years and counting, and will continue doing so for as long as I live.

Key Takeaways:

If you find the love of your life and choose to get married, write your own vows for your wedding.

Make this special moment something to remember every day from that day forward. Make it visible, have it in your room so you both can see it.

Songs:

"I Do" – Colbie Caillat

"Would You Go with Me" – Josh Turner

"You Decorated My Life" – Kenny Rogers

"I Want Crazy" – Hunter Hays

"Para Amarnos Más" – Mijares

"Todo Cambió" – Camila

"Para Siempre" – Kany Garcia

"A Fuego Lento" – Rosana

"Algo Contigo" – Rita Payes, Elisabeth Roma

We Are Equal, but We Are Not the Same

*"In marriage if both of you were the same,
one of you would be unnecessary."* – Tony Evans

I've always found it disrespectful that still on some invitations to special events (weddings, graduations, anniversaries, etc.) the envelope says: "Mr. and Mrs...." followed by the man's full name. I do not believe it is right to erase a woman's identity; is it too hard to write both names in the same envelope? If the intent is to extend the invitation for the person and a guest, then just put the name of the person and add an extra ticket to the event or say "plus one" as many invitations already do. If someone knows the name of the person they are inviting, I guarantee they know or for sure can find out the full name of their spouse. A bit more effort and a little more ink would not hurt anyone and would show the respect each person deserves.

The example of the invitation to an event is just the symptom, not the root cause of my discomfort with the real issue. The real issue is the social convention that upon marriage, a woman should change her last name and adopt the last name of her husband. I find this completely outdated. Still in some countries, women not only change their last name, but also add the term "De" to their new last name which in Spanish translates "of" that new family. You would say "Marisela Ramos De Leon" in the case of my wife. This makes it sound like the woman was "acquired" by the man upon marriage. I understand that historically that might not have been solely the intent, and I respect those who believe that is important for their family lineage. Likewise, I am not going to debate all the meaning or value attributed to the tradition of a dowry payment made by the bride's family to the groom's family at the time of marriage. With an eye of openness, I want to believe that the true intent was to help the newlyweds to start their life together with support from their families, as traditionally the man would come to the marriage with his "fortune" (however grand or scarce it might have been), intrinsically associated with his family's assets, and in turn, the woman would join the marriage bringing her own share of assets to add to the new couple's wealth.

As you will read later in this book, I am a believer in supporting our kids throughout life so I would not be opposed to a concept like this if that was its truly pure intention. Today it might be transformed from a dowry to a rather handsome gift from the parents of either of the newlyweds, in many different shapes and forms, and that is totally fine with me.

That is not truly the issue in question, the issue for me continues being the change in last name by social convention. I still believe that not only is it antiquated, but in my view, it does not honor or equally respect both people in a marriage and I think that newly formed couples more and more are opting out from that and choosing their couple's identity.

Additionally, it does not recognize the fact that in this day and age, the definition of a traditional marriage and a traditional family has evolved. With same sex couples getting married, with families that have women being the lead provider for financial stability, and a whole new configuration of family arrangements, the traditional set up of one person taking the last name of the other one, like "Mr. and Mrs. last name" needs to change and should not be determined by any societal expectation. At the end, it is only up to each couple to decide about their own identity.

In our marriage, we both decided there was no change in names. We both are clear on our identities and very proud of our family names as well. So, we agreed that each of us would keep our original names as we came into our marriage, as that is what each of us brought to the relationship, equally, and we wanted to keep it that way.

We get a kick out of all kinds of silly situations where I get called "Mr. Ramos" or my wife is called "Mrs. Leon". We still see eyebrows lift when we check into a hotel and the front desk clerk sees we have different last names, and it certainly takes extra work and explaining when we are doing renewal of passports, visas, changes of countries, etc. But "simplifying" paperwork is not a good reason to change who you are and to not honor your heritage.

We also decided to extend this opportunity to honor all our heritage to our kids. We decided to pass both of our last names to them. They are not just "León". They are "León-Ramos", together, joined as we are. They have the best of each one of us, so they deserve to have their heritage from both families. This is our gift to them, it is who they are, and we are very proud of it.

Key Takeaways:

If you are fortunate to find the love of your life, your "forever person" and choose to get married, don't just go with a social convention like changing last names upon marriage without questioning your beliefs on the matter.

This is only for the couple to decide according to their own values. It is their own identity as a newly formed family.

Songs:

"Reflections of Passion" – Yanni

"Little Things" – One Direction

A Very Special Welcome!

"A baby is God's way to tell us
that life should go on." – Robert Brault

I've read that waiting for something that you really want develops your cerebral prefrontal cortex, which allows you to make more thoughtful and well considered choices, rather than acting on immediate desires alone. The idea of delayed gratification enables a person to prioritize long-term goals, which is crucial for achieving significant aspirations.

Waiting for Christmas, for your birthday, for summer vacations, waiting to visit friends or loved ones that we don't see often, and many other things can become significant ways to train yourself in this area but, in my experience, nothing compares to waiting for the arrival of a new baby to the family. Let me tell you, if your cerebral prefrontal cortex is not fully developed yet, it will be as you go through this experience.

As parents, the wait starts from the moment you desire to have a family. All the conversations about it, all the planning, the actual "trying" and the excitement of waiting to see the result of those pregnancy tests certainly make your heart skip a bit many times. For some people this wait can be several months long, for others, it can be years, and for some, it may never come.

If you are blessed with having one child, and you decide to expand your family, how you wait for each child is different in many ways. While the preparation steps can be similar (the doctor visits, the pre-natal courses, getting the new baby room ready, the baby showers, the hospital, etc), many other things are unique for each baby. For instance, the wait for a first child has a lot of unknowns and like any first-time parent, we all tend to overdo things a little bit, just to be on the safe side. Then as you have the second and third child, many things are familiar but the family dynamic changes as the attention and needs multiply exponentially. In particular, the arrival of the second and third child (and beyond, for those that venture into having larger families) involves the first and second children (and so on) being aware and involved in the waiting period. Having them actively participate and getting excited about their new baby siblings is something very important to the entire family.

There are so many ways you can involve the kids in waiting for their new siblings to arrive, like talking or singing to the unborn baby, feeling the kicks of the baby on the mother's belly and other ideas around going together to shop for things for the new baby and helping with the preparation of their room and the house. It does not take a genius to realize the risk that we all run to focus too much on the new baby at the expense of the older kids in the family.

The arrival of the first baby is always unique. Parents and the baby are new to the experience, and in our case, for the arrival of Andrea, our first child, the entire family (grandparents, uncles, aunts, and most of our friends) made their debut in their roles at the same time for the first time. All kinds of gifts and demonstrations of love poured down to the family and to our baby daughter Andrea. It was explosive and emotionally charged for everyone!

When we had Fernando (our second baby) and Rodrigo (our third baby), my wife came up with a couple of rituals that made it very special for the older siblings. The first one was at the moment of birth of the new baby. As Fernando was born, she arranged to have a basket of toys in the hospital room and also at home when we returned. When visitors came with a gift for Fernando's birth, we handed them a gift to give to Andrea, our oldest child.

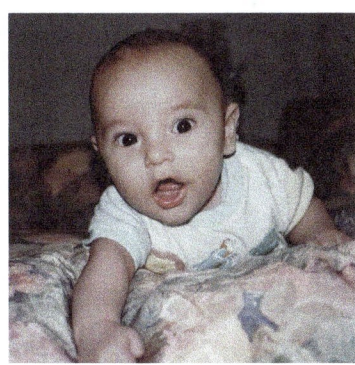

So, every time she saw anyone bringing a gift to the new baby, she received a gift as well. We did the same when Rodrigo was born, so both Andrea and Fernando received gifts on his arrival. This made it very special for the siblings, as most of the attention went to the new baby, they also felt cared for in a way that was meaningful to them.

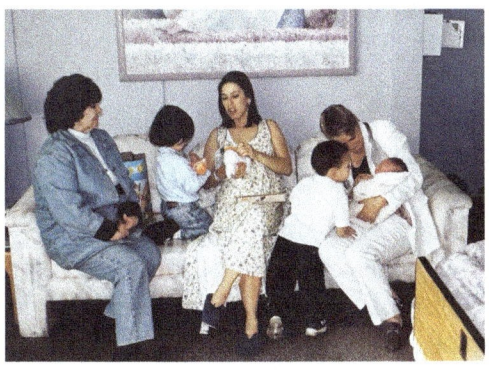
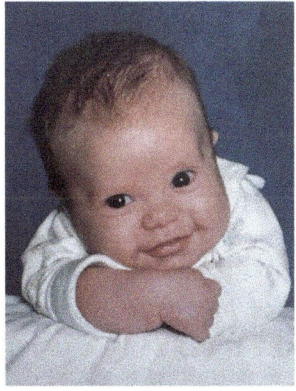

The second ritual was an activity that became a core memory for Fernando. Right after Rodrigo was born, due to my job we moved from Mexico City to Phoenix, Arizona. We moved to another country for the first time, with three young kids (Andrea was 4, Fernando was 2 and Rodrigo was 45 days old). As you can imagine this brought a lot of change at the same time: changing home, school, language, weather, leaving family and friends and whatever semblance of stability for our still young family unit. Out of all the family members, Fernando was experiencing a harder time. Andrea coped faster at school, it could have been that by the time she was 4 years old, this was her 3rd move, and being a bit older, she had the benefit of understanding a little more what was going on.

At the other end, Rodrigo, being just 45 days old, had no idea of what was going on, or the magnitude of the change. For him, this was the beginning of his family life. Fernando is the one who had the rug pulled out from under his feet. Suddenly, he had all these changes thrust upon him, having a baby brother that needed a lot of attention, and he was going to a new day care, in another place, in another language, surrounded by strange people, without any of his extended family members around.

We noticed how he needed a bit more support to cope with all the changes happening in his life. Among many things we did to help him, my wife came up with a brilliant idea for a ritual. She found a beautiful lake near our home that had ducks, birds and walking paths. She took Fernando there one day and told him this was their "secret place" just for him and her. This was something that was not for his siblings, it was just for him. They went to this place regularly, walked, played, fed the ducks, and just sat there enjoying their time together, with no one else. I believe this ritual made a huge difference in Fernando's well-being and self-confidence. To this day, when he is 27 years old, he vividly remembers his special place with his Mom and cherishes those moments spent together.

Our learning is simple. Give each kid what they need, when they need it, and how they need it. Having gifts for them upon the

arrival of a sibling was a wonderful way to have good news for everyone. Having a special place, just for one of them when he needed it, was a magnificent way to give him the bonding and undivided attention he needed.

Key Takeaways:

The waiting period for a new baby to be born is a unique window of time that won't be repeated for that child and for their siblings (if there are any). Make them part of it as frequently as possible and make them feel as special as the new baby when they arrive.

When a new baby is born, every member of the family is adjusting, especially little siblings. No matter how complex or hectic life with a new baby can be, always find the time and priority to give each child what they need, when they need it and how they need it.

Songs:

"Duerme" – Jack Rabbit
"You'll Be in My Heart" – Phil Collins
"Bubbly" – Colby Caillat
"God Must Have Spent a Little More Time on You" – NSYNC

Common Objectives – for Us and for the Kids

"If the family were a boat,
it would be a canoe that makes no progress
unless everyone paddles." – Letty Cottin Pogrebin

Being a Human Resources leader for most of my professional career, I know what makes an effective team, and more importantly, I know what makes a happy team. While there are many factors that contribute, like having a great leader, good relationships and good communication, the most important factor is having trust in each other and working towards a meaningful common objective, with a clear direction and with a personal, emotional and rational connection to the team's purpose. That is what brings a team together and enables them to thrive.

Our family is a team and as such, it is paramount that we trust each other and find our collective purpose, as well as to discover, define and share common objectives. It cannot be the objectives of the parents imposed on their children. Sure, when they are very little, parents have the responsibility to steer the family team in the right direction but as the kids grow, even from a very early age, they have their own voice, interests, and wants, which need to be considered as that will enrich the family and bring higher satisfaction.

Just as it is very important for an individual to have clarity on their own purpose, values and principles, it is vital for a family to talk about what binds them together and the things they value the most. It can be done in many ways, from talking about it on a family dinner, perhaps on a holiday or special occasion, to facilitating activities that can lead to producing a document or something more structured, it all depends on each family style.

For instance, in our family, my wife found a poster with a set of family principles that we believed represented behaviors we wanted to adopt. We talked about it as a family, to understand what they meant to each one and posted them on a door that we all go through every day before we leave the house.

This has served for many years as a reminder of the behaviors we want to practice in our interactions as a family on a daily basis and how we want to show up to the world.

Like anything in life, most of what we learn is through repetition, so my wife and I constantly make explicit reminders of these principles. From very simple things like "Always say please and thank you" to "In our family we share things" to every day reminding them when they go to school "Be nice and play fair" and "Do your best", "Have Fun", "Never Give Up" and "Always tell the truth".

And we always remind all of us to "Laugh often", "Pay with Hugs and Kisses" and end pretty much every conversation saying "I love you" every time. You will see many of these principles shared in greater detail throughout this book.

These principles / behaviors are great for day-to-day interactions, to be congruent with our values as a family, in a similar way as any team (sports, corporate, non-profit, education, etc) would have their operating principles or team norms to be congruent with their values.

An Intentional Family's Love Story

When I think about common objectives for a family, the most important thing is that they mean something for every family member, that there is something in it for each person to pursue and participate fully engaged. It is a precious activity to learn how to set common objectives as a family as it involves working together as a team, listening to each other, making decisions together, learning to negotiate, understanding the motivations of each family member and ultimately getting everyone to rally behind the family's common objective. It can be practiced with simple things such as having a family night, a family weekend, a vacation, a special trip, etc. And it goes on to bigger things like moving to another city/country, supporting a family member through a tough situation, and how to get out of a family conflict.

I believe this is one of the most basic and most important concepts parents can teach their kids, to set goals, to be part of a loving, collaborative and high-performing family unit, where each member cares for the rest and support each other to achieve the collective purpose and to elevate each family member to achieve their own personal aspirations. And it is one of the main reasons why families can continue to be present, even when every family member is an adult, and all have their own families. Finding that common objective, that special project, that moment that brings the "team" together to collaborate, is what counts. It can be a family reunion, to celebrate a grandparent's special birthday, to do a grownup's trip...the trick is to not just stay with our ordinary routines...find a special goal and talk as a family, make it a common objective and once accomplished, find the next one!

In our family an example of finding common objectives is traveling together. It can go anywhere from a nearby day trip to an international trip. And we have made this an experience of defining and living our common objectives as a family. I talk more about this in the chapter of "Oh the places we go!"

For those families that want to go deeper into developing their purpose, I recommend reading Chapter 2 of **The 7 Habits of Highly Effective Families** by Stephen R. Covey, where he talks about Habit #2: Begin with the End in Mind — Bringing Purpose and Vision to Your Family.

Key Takeaways:

Your family is the most important team you will ever belong to. Be intentional in creating your family purpose, values, principles and goals.

Involve and engage all family members on "family projects" like you would do at work. Planning things together and sharing responsibilities will create very special memories.

Song:

"A Million Dreams" – Lucy Thomas

Our Family Language

"Love will find its way
through all languages on its own." - Rumi

If trust and having common objectives are the cornerstone of a team, or a family, having a common language, a family code, is a fun way to make the family have their own character, flair, and fun. The common language and code come from spending time together, having shared experiences, moments that we all enjoy and things we only know. It is that "secret handshake" that only those belonging to a very special club know.

In our family, some of the common languages come from our family movie nights, when we watched something together, in many cases over and over again. For example, I am a lifelong fan of the sit-com **Friends**, and I watch it constantly, with my wife, and with our kids when they were the appropriate age to understand it. By doing so, I guess I passed that onto the family, we all speak the "**Friends** language", and we can certainly find a quote from **Friends** for everyday situations in our lives. The particular show is not what is important, it is the connection that is formed when we remember something we watched together.

We also have a very particular family whistle. We use it when we get home, when we want to grab someone's attention at a public place, instead of yelling their name, we whistle. It is unique, and it is ours. We also have the dance language, as we have been dancing for years. When we get together, just for dinner, or at any special event, there is music and there is dancing! Magic happens when you communicate as a family dancing together, singing the songs, following the moves, and just having fun in our very own particular way.

We have the language of music, those songs that remind us of our special bond, the values we share, how much we miss our home when we are not there, our family, our time together. This is why you will see recommended songs in every chapter of this book. Music is part of our family love language.

And we have the language of hugs, we crawl up on a couch, on a bed, altogether and hug each other. No matter whatever it is, every family needs a common language, or many common languages. This is how we express our bond, we are a tribe, we are unique and we belong together.

Key Takeaways:

All families have their very special languages. Learn what your family languages are. Be explicit, talk about them with your family so all members know and appreciate them.

Foster using them constantly, even as the kids grow up and leave home. You are never too old to do your "secret handshake" with your kids.

Songs:

"Home" – Michael Bubble
"Lost" – Michael Bubble
"Have It All" – Jason Mraz
"Lucky" – Jason Mraz, Colby Caillat
"I Hope You Dance" – Lee Ann Womack
"Sin Miedo" – Rosana
"Color Esperanza" – Diego Torres
"I Could Not Ask for More" – Edwin McCain
"Back Home" – Andy Grammer

Dinner Together, Movies, Walks to the Park

"Enjoy the little things in life, for one day you will realize they were the big things." – Robert Brault

Many daily routines in any family can turn into very special moments of connection for all members. A routine activity such as having a meal can become precious if it has meaning for those who share it. It is just a matter of adding a few ingredients and we can turn any routine into a memorable family ritual.

It is not necessarily the movie watched, or the food that was eaten, or whatever was happening at the park that day. It was the time we were together, the moments when we talked about life, and we shared our time, we shared our lives. So, when you have the opportunity to do them, think about three things: 1) Be fully present, give your undivided attention to the moment, don't multitask or worry about tomorrow, or think about work, don't let the phone distract you, or anyone steal the moment away, 2) Do it often, don't worry about having a great plan, just do it, as often as you can, 3) Make it memorable, create a ritual that is simple and easy to do and remember.

One of the most important and impactful activities that a family can do together is to sit down to share their meals. Our human biological construct has given us the wonderful opportunity of needing to eat three times per day. I strongly believe that at a minimum, all families need to have at least one meal a day together. When you live in a family setting, these opportunities cannot be wasted by having each member eat at a different time, alone, or rush down, grab something and go out the door, or come home after school or work, grab something and go to their room, or make a habit of going to the drive-thru and scarfing something down in the car a few times per week. It also cannot be wasted by being together but not being fully present, by not engaging with other family members. It is in these moments of sitting down by the table, facing each other, expressing our gratitude for having something to eat, sharing things, passing things, talking about the day, asking about each other, where a family root and bond is being built, one bite at a time, one meal at a time.

For instance, at our family dinners we have two rituals. One is a very simple review of the day that starts by Mom asking a question: "What is your High and Low of the day?" and someone volunteers to share and then the rest follow. From our kids being very little to now when they are grown adults, whenever we share a dinner, we will have a "High and Low" of the day ritual. You would be surprised how much we have shared and learned with that simple question.

The second ritual is when we have a meal after sharing some activities together, like when we travel together, we will do a review of what we experienced together, and we will ask to give a "Thumbs Up, Thumbs Neutral, or Thumbs Down" to rate the activity. The trick is that we all put our hands in front at the same time and either Mom or Dad asks, "So, what is your feedback to the activity?" and a quick drum roll ensues and then everyone displays their thumb response at the same time. Then we talk about what we liked or not about the activity. This makes everyone present to discuss the same topic and creates an opportunity to relive the experience.

Another beautiful little daily ritual was the moment I returned home from work. My wife made it very special. No matter if I just returned from any day at the office, or if I returned from a long business trip, she would find a way to greet me at the door, give me a 20 second hug and walk with me inside to talk about our day. As we started having kids, she brought them into this "Daddy is home" ritual as often as possible. As she knew my car was parking, she would rally the kids to run to the door to greet me, jumping and saying, "Daddy is home!" You feel like a rock star at home! And more importantly, you feel loved. No matter what my day had, my mood was immediately lifted and my load taken off my shoulders. To this day, as our kids are not home anymore, she continues to practice the ritual of greeting me home at the door when I arrive after being away with a big hug and a kiss and it is very special to me.

Let me tell you that when the kids grow, and move out of the house, the things you miss the most are those simple, daily routines and moments of interaction together. The dinner every night, the movie nights, the walks to the park, the "Daddy is home" welcome. They are not gone; they just happen less frequently now. Those are precious foundations, moments where relationships are built, moments where lifetime, core memories are created and shared. What makes them so memorable is the opportunity to be present in each other's lives.

The beautiful thing about these simple rituals is that any family member can carry them forward as the grown kids move and start their new families. And as a parent, you can find opportunities to do it again, when you get together to remember special moments and to create new memories in every stage of life.

Key Takeaways:

Make an absolute priority for your family to eat together, at least one meal a day, being fully present.

Set the example with your actions. Give your undivided attention to your family at this moment. Whatever you do, the family will do as well.

Make it a ritual, simple, fun and engage everyone. Try different things, find your own thing, make it stick by being consistent.

Songs:

"The Best Day (Taylor's Version)" – Taylor Swift

"Days Like This" – Busby Marou

Driving to Places, Driving Togetherness

"Good company in a journey
makes the way seem shorter."- Izaak Walton

In our modern times, we spend a considerable amount of time in a vehicle, going places, and when it comes to having a family, this also becomes a daily routine. In my view, this is not just a means of getting from A to B, in many ways, it can be very valuable time spent together. Where else can you get your kids voluntarily (most of the time) in a confined space, safely restrained (by a safety belt), with the rest of the family members for long periods of time?

If you are intentional and play your cards correctly, this could become a priceless family ritual. When the kids are little, it is an opportunity to listen to music, sing, and learn a bit more from them every day. The temptation to just hook the kids with an iPad, or vehicle entertainment system, can be detrimental to the family's communication, and a waste of precious time together. Some families do have the ritual of planning road trips for special vacations or to go visit family or friends, move the kids to college, or other special occasions. Why not have the same intentionality to plan a daily road trip to school or to after-school activities?

My wife is very smart about this. When the kids were little, she incorporated music, singing, spotting objects with games like "I see...", going to special places for them as part of the route, and it also allowed for time to talk about their day in the daily commutes. As our kids grew, she always favored doing something together vs. abdicating to technology and default to isolation of family members in the car. It is not easy, and certainly kids do not always cooperate, but some of those activities have now become a precious memory for them as they have grown. Now that they are adults, invariably and regularly each one of them calls my wife during their long commutes or when stuck in traffic and they continue to talk about their lives, and it is a memorable ritual that has been kept as a family bond even though we don't live in the same city, and we don't drive together often. She is now harvesting the bounty of all the beautiful seeds she planted earlier in their lives.

Key Takeaway:

If you are going to be driving your kids everywhere for many years, don't dread it, enjoy it, make it fun, make it memorable, make it an opportunity to learn about your kids, to build a stronger connection.

Songs:

"El Taqui Taqui (Original Mix)" – Ilegales

"Ultimate" – Lindsay Lohan

"Viva la Vida" – Coldplay

"Iko, Iko (My Bestie)" – Justin Wellington, Small Jam

Happy Birthday and "Las Mañanitas"

"Your birthday is the day the universe decided
it could no longer go on without YOU!"

Of all the ways one can celebrate a birthday, in my view, nothing can replace the beautiful sound of the voices of your loved ones being around and singing a happy birthday and cheering you on for another great year in your life.

As family members grow, move on, go away, relocate, or simply go on with their adult lives, getting together for every birthday is more complex. One tradition in our families is to sing "Las Mañanitas" (by Alfonso Esparza Oteo) which translates to "Early Little Mornings" in English, which is like a happy birthday song in Spanish. The difference is that the lyrics of the song in Spanish are all about singing early in the morning as a way to wake up the person and express your love for them.

Las Mañanitas (Spanish)

Estas son las mañanitas que cantaba el rey David,
hoy por ser día de tu santo te las cantamos aquí,

Despierta, mi bien, despierta, mira que ya amaneció,
ya los pajaritos cantan, la luna ya se metió,

Qué linda está la mañana en que vengo a saludarte,
venimos todos con gusto y placer a felicitarte,

El día en que tu naciste, nacieron todas las flores.
Y en la pila del bautismo, cantaron los ruiseñores,

Ya viene amaneciendo, ya la luz del día nos dio,
Levántate de mañana, mira que ya amaneció,

Si yo pudiera bajarte las estrellas y un lucero,
para poder demostrarte lo mucho que yo te quiero,

Con jazmines y flores, este día quiero adornar,
Hoy, por ser día de tu santo, te venimos a cantar

Las Mañanitas (English)

These are the little mornings, that king David used to sing,
because today is your birthday, we sign them to you here,

Wake up, my dear, wake up, see that it is already dawn,
the little birds are already singing, and the moon has already set,

What a beautiful morning in which I come to greet you,
we all come with joy and pleasure to congratulate you,

The day you were born, all flowers were born.
And at the baptismal font, the nightingales sang,

It is starting to dawn, and the daylight is on us,
Get up in the morning, and see that it has already dawned,

If I could bring down the stars and a morning star,
to show how much I love you,

With jasmines and flowers, I want to decorate this day,
Today, on your birthday, we all come to sing to you

This has a very special meaning, as you want the person to know how much you love them and your best wishes for their special day as early as possible in the day. The family tradition is to sing together "las mañanitas" very early, regardless of wherever any member of the family might be around the world. This is not exclusive to our family, for instance, in my wife's family, they even have a running competition to see who is the first one to call whomever birthday is that day. And they end up calling each other very early in the morning just to get the bragging rights of being the first to call whoever's birthday was that day.

In our family given we have lived in different cities and sometimes different countries at a time, we do this via the phone/Facetime/ WhatsApp. No matter the time zone difference, we coordinate so we all call early in the morning at the location of the family member whose birthday is. It is important to have video so we can see everyone, no matter how you look, no need to dress up, no need to put on make-up or anything, and more importantly, so everyone singing can see the face of the one being celebrated when they hear the song and wake up remembering it is their birthday and the very first thing they receive that day is the love of their family with a very special wake-up call.

The idea is to do it in the very same way we would do it if we were all living at the same place, where we would silently approach together the room of the family member whose birthday is that day, and would sing "Las Mañanitas" and jump on the bed to shower them with hugs and kisses before sharing any kind of gifts, cards or even a small cake to blow a candle.

Being myself a recipient of so many "Las Mañanitas", most of them live with the presence of my wife and kids, and a few virtually given all the moves and travel that we have done, I can tell you it is wonderful to start your birthday listening to the voices and seeing the faces of the people you love the most in life. This is priceless and a cherished tradition that we continue to carry on.

Key Takeaways:

Every birthday is a wonderful moment for each member of the family and for all. Regardless of the busy schedules, locations where we live, or complexities of our daily lives, we can make a priority to get together, physically or virtually to celebrate our loved ones on that special day.

Do it early in the morning, bringing the family together to celebrate in a special way the start of their day for the person you love.

Songs:

"Las Mañanitas" – Mariachi Vargas de Tecalitlán

"Las Mañanitas" – Tatiana

"Happy Birthday To You" – Happy Occasion Singers

"Parabéns pra Você" - SaraoMusic

Celebrating Moments & Milestones
with Toasts and Speeches

"The more you praise and celebrate your life, the more there is in life to celebrate." - Oprah

Once I heard a story about the meaning of clinking glasses when making a toast that made a lot of sense to me. It is done because that brings all of our 5 senses into the moment. We can see the drink, appreciate the colors, how it moves, how light reflects through the glass and into the liquid; we can smell it, perceive the aroma and distinguish the different traces of ingredients as we inhale deeper; we can feel it when we take the first sip as it touches our lips, as it goes into our mouth we can feel the texture; we can taste it, identifying different flavors, if it is sweet, sour, salty, fruity or just plain as water; and finally we can also hear it when we clink the glasses, so the experience is complete. When all your senses are focused on the same thing at the same time, you elevate your awareness of the moment and enjoy the here and now, being fully present, consciously.

In my view, being fully present focused on your drink when making a toast is just the preamble of the holistic human experience of celebrating something. In addition to the wine or whatever drink you prefer, and the glasses used to hold it, what makes the moment really special are three things: 1) The reason for the celebration, 2) The people gathered to celebrate, and 3) The feelings shared during the celebration. This last reason is where a toast becomes such an important part of any celebration. This makes it a ritual; it makes it memorable.

In our family, celebrations and toasts are a cherished tradition where the entire family joins, on many special occasions. Be it a new year's toast, a family member's special birthday, graduation, or even a very special family moment (a vacation, a trip, a family reunion). This is a tradition that my wife brought from her family, where her father would usually bring everyone together and will start asking someone (usually my wife) to get the toast started. Once my wife makes a toast, her siblings one by one would follow, then the spouses and kids of any age would also participate. We value every family member's participation, no matter how little they are. We take the time to hear from each one who wants to say a few words. It is a beautiful experience to see all the little kids of the family participate, at first saying a few funny words and as they grow, start expressing their own voice, and expressing their own personality.

Beyond the lovely feeling as a family, this is also a safe, nurturing environment to build self-confidence, to share their voice with adults and learn how to interact in a social setting. For kids to watch and listen to all the beautiful words shared about a special occasion creates a stronger sense of belonging to the family. The trick is to be intentional and patient. Intentional by inviting every family member to participate, to learn how to express their feelings saying a few words and being patient and caring about what each one shares, without judgement, without expecting a marvelous speech from anyone.

This is about family sharing, not an oratory contest. The ultimate goal is to create a sense of shared appreciation and gratitude, to express our love for each other in whatever way each family member can. Seeing a little kid stand up, hold their juice cup up and say a few words, having the undivided attention and support of the entire family, learning how to feel confident to share feelings with a group, and speaking their minds is invaluable.

I believe this is a way to also help kids gain confidence speaking in public in a setting where they can be vulnerable, where they know everyone around the table loves them and no matter what they say, it will be well received, with love and appreciation for their participation.

It has been a wonderful experience to witness the evolution of the skills of our kids when giving their toasts within our family setting and beyond when we've had graduations and other large family and friends' events. Many times, they come prepared for the occasion, with their key thoughts captured on their iPhones, and many others they just improvise, sharing what they feel in the moment, speaking from their hearts.

 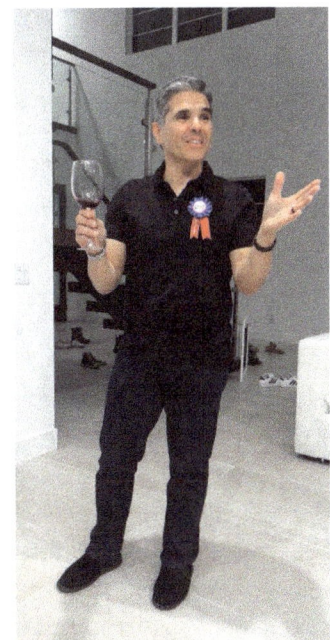

Key Takeaways:

When you celebrate a special occasion, have a toast, say what you feel and invite other family members to do the same.

Bring the kids along, have them participate, let them share how they feel, in their own words. Be patient, encourage them and make them feel special by having a voice in every meaningful celebration.

Song:

"What a Wonderful World" – Louis Armstrong

"Concrete Hands" and Home is Where Your Heart Is

"A house is made with walls and beams;
a home is built with love and dreams." – Ralph Waldo Emerson

Because of my job in an international company, as a family we moved homes 14 times, having the opportunity to live in 4 different countries. It has been a wonderful experience in many ways. Our three kids, Andrea, Fernando and Rodrigo, learned what it means to leave a home and go to a new one, multiple times, at a very early age. Our youngest son Rodrigo's first international move was when he was 45 days old!

Given that all those moves were associated with my job, we knew our stay was always temporary, until the assignment was complete (usually in 2 to 3 yrs) and then off we went to another job assignment. This temporary nature made our kids ask us on several occasions "Where is home?" "Is it Mexico, where we were born?", "Is it Mason, Ohio, where we lived more years as a family?" and the answer we gave them was "home is where your heart is, it is where the family is at that moment. The house, the walls, the furniture, the things we have, are all temporary. What makes a home is the love we have, the experiences we share, the time and the moments we are together."

In one of our moves back to Cincinnati we decided to build our home. For the first time in our almost 20 years of marriage at the time, we had the opportunity to not rent, or to buy an existing house. It was our opportunity to build the "house of our dreams", to fit our family needs. We built it in Mason, Ohio, a typical Midwest suburb where a standard pattern of home construction and design was kind of expected. We decided to break the mold and build a contemporary home, unique, very colorful, very different.

We got our fair share of criticism and complaints voiced from some random neighbors to the homeowner's association (HOA). We also got a lot of praise from other close neighbors, friends and strangers who embraced something different. We did everything the right way, all designs, materials, colors, and specifications were duly approved at the time of construction by the developers and the HOA when we started the process. But the fact that it looked very different from the norm ended up polarizing those who saw it, either by those living nearby, or those who drove by our house.

We designed every detail to our own taste, both on the inside and outside. We also were able to have a very special family ritual during the construction process, to imprint all our family hands together at the driveway when the contractor was pouring the concrete:

This became a way to stamp our family seal into our first home ever. I tell this story because having such a customized house is not what truly matters. As much as we love the design, and how functional it is as it suits our needs, that is not what is most important. What matters most are all the moments we live and share together there. Upon finalizing construction, we were very fortunate to have lived there altogether for 6 years, the longest time we've been in any place. This was the place where each of our kids lived during most or through all of their high school years before moving to college. And those "concrete hands" got to see each one of them leaving. We also know that like any other home, this is temporary.

Now our kids live in Los Angeles, California, and wherever we are, we continue believing and saying "home is where our hearts are, where our family is together at that moment", sometimes it is there in California, other times it is this house, and in the future, it might be somewhere else. What truly matters is that we can get together to be reunited, to remember and celebrate our shared experiences and continue filling our home with new memories.

Key Takeaways:

The difference between a house, no matter how customized or humble it might be, and a home is the love of the family that lives there, the moments shared together there.

Don't get attached to things or places. Everything is temporary. Enjoy wherever you are, home is wherever your family can be together.

Songs:

"Home – Phillip Phillips

"Que No Falte Hogar" – *Eduardo Ortiz Tirado, Cantantes Inhumyc*

The Red Frisbee

"A father can play like a kid, give advice like a friend and protect like a bodyguard." - Unknown

Playing catch with your little kids is a wonderful experience and it is something that cannot be substituted by any video game or technological advance. It is a moment when a parent and a child give their undivided attention to the moment, to each other.

It can come in many ways, it can be throwing a ball, playing basketball, kicking a soccer ball, playing ping-pong or tennis, jogging or running track, doing yoga, dancing together, etc. The important thing is that it involves three things: 1) it is between two people (you can also have one or two more sometimes if there are other siblings), 2) it is outdoors, in nature, and 3) it is not a match/not competitive, that is not the goal. The ulterior purpose of playing catch is the bonding that takes place between a parent and a child by spending time together, having the opportunity to talk to each other.

The bonding starts not when you are throwing the ball, it starts when both the parent and the child talk about spending time together, making it a priority and deciding to be with each other. There are precious moments, before you start, during and after the activity where you talk about stuff, you relax your mind from your daily commitments and pressures, and get into the moment, talk about the last time you did this, have you improved your throw, do you have any new moves, etc. And that opens the door to talk about other things, and take interest in their lives, their friends, their problems and...do your thing, as a parent.

The other beautiful thing about playing catch is that you cannot throw and catch a ball with an iPhone in your hand, you must commit to the moment and be present. When I saw the benefits and enjoyment of this activity, I thought about a way to be able to do it as much as possible with my kids. So, I bought a very light, flexible red frisbee. I carry it around whenever we travel or go out for a day trip or just whenever we go out as a family. I can put it in my briefcase, backpack, even in my wife's purse. When we arrive at the park, beach, backyard, front street, driveway and even sometimes in parking lots or basically anywhere, I could pull out my red frisbee and have a moment to connect with my kids. Sometimes we just played for a few minutes, and some other times we spent a lot of time throwing it back and forth, laughing and talking about stuff. I started when they were very little, and I still do it with them now that they are adults. The moment I pull the red frisbee, I see one of them running and saying: "Papi, throw it to me…" and there we go…

Recently I got to see the power of this concept at another level. My wife and I started to volunteer at an association called "Saturday Hoops" whose purpose is to help improve kids' outlook on life and on themselves by inspiring them to try new things and make new friends. The concept is very simple, they invite kids and volunteers to play sports, do arts and crafts, reading and other things together on Saturday mornings.

On the sports activities, there is nothing fancy, no uniforms, no referees, just "pick-up" play like you would be playing amongst friends or neighbors at the park. The kids and volunteers mix organically into teams and start playing sports together. When you play sports, you start communicating to pass the ball, to plan the next play, to celebrate a goal scored, when you are waiting on the sideline for your teams' turn to return to the field, and little by little you start opening up to talk about other things in their life that can trigger an opportunity to initiate a mentoring relationship that can make a difference with kids who need guidance and support.

This experience reinforced my belief in how important the role of sports and playing with someone they can look up to for the development of a child can be. By investing time together with someone they respect and see as a role model in any area of their lives, it makes kids feel loved, important and confident.

Key Takeaways:

Make a habit of playing sports or doing physical activity with your kids, preferably one-on-one.

Do what they like doing, not what you like doing. Do it as often as you can and as often as they want. Continue doing it when they are adults.

Engage not only in physical activity, talk about the plan to do the activity, talk about their lives, ask questions, and spend time together after the activity.

Songs:

"You've Got a Friend in Me" – Randy Newman
"With Arms Wide Open" - Creed

The Sand Pyramid

"Like a sandcastle, all is temporary. Build it, tend it, enjoy it.
And when the time comes, let it go." – Jack Kornfield

There are not many activities in life as relaxing as playing in the sand, in whatever form you prefer. The setting is designed by nature to slow down, to be present and feel the moment. The clear water, the blue sky, the sunshine, the soft breeze, the waves coming in and out with their white crests and rhythmic sound, in a never-ending teasing dance with the shore. No matter what anyone's state of mind is, when we all get to a beach, we take a deep breath, smile and want to go for a walk, put our feet in the water, perhaps jump into the waves, or simply just sit down, lay down and take in all of nature's healing and loving energy.

In my case, I like to do all of the above with the exception of laying down. When I am at the beach, I like to be active, practice sports and play in the sand, with my feet, with my hands, just feeling a different texture that I don't get to enjoy on a regular basis. Many other people do the same, and I can bet that on all visits to a beach, we will always see a sandcastle being built. This is one of the most fun things anyone can do at any age.

Many years ago, I initiated a ritual of building a Sand Pyramid, instead of a sandcastle. Being Mexican, I thought this could be a fun thing to do for a few reasons. The first one is that it is simpler to build and anyone can do it. You do not need any instruments, buckets, shovels or anything, just your bare hands. The second and more important one, it gave me an opportunity to talk to our kids about the pyramids, which is something very important in our cultural heritage. Finally, it draws the attention of people around as anyone walking by would stop and ask "what are you building?" and we would engage in a conversation, meet people, and many times would recruit additional helpers.

Now every time we go to the beach, our kids know and expect that we will build a sand pyramid together. It has become a ritual that, in a very tangential way, keeps them connected to their Mexican heritage. I do believe that somehow, we must have in our ancestry a trace back to someone who either helped build the pyramids or saw them, or lived near them, or simply was part of that culture when they were at their peak of magnificence.

Speaking of sharing our Mexican cultural heritage with our kids, there are so many things to write about that it is impossible to do justice in just one story or even in one book. I just want to say that in our family roots, it is very important to frequently do things similar to the sand-pyramid. When you live abroad and are far removed from your native culture, the responsibility is on the parents to find opportunities to remind the entire family where they come from and to do it in a way that helps them remember something important about who they are.

In our family we always celebrate all the Mexican holidays and the most festive year-round traditions in parallel to the holidays and traditions of the countries where we lived when we were there. Whenever possible, we get together with other friends and family, we dress up with the national colors, we cook the good stuff, we play the music and dance to the rhythms of our culture as frequently as possible. We root for the national teams and athletes, no matter if they win or lose, and we keep our language, jokes and slang alive and well so our kids will never forget and can belong as much as possible when we can visit the country.

All of these rituals and traditions strengthen the connection of our family with our cultural roots. And these are usually what are most obvious and visible to everyone, even outside our family and friends. In many ways, the colors of a flag, the national team jersey, the chants and all the traditional year-round celebrations are what you would usually expect to see in a family with Mexican heritage.

There is another dimension that our Mexican heritage has which I also find very meaningful, and it is to connect with the wisdom of our ancestors. Every culture has it in the form of philosophy, teachings, quotes, sayings, and other types of popular knowledge that are transferred down through generations. While neither my wife nor I are experts or historians in this subject, many times we would remember a saying or quote in a particular situation and we make sure to explain to our kids where it came from and to this day, we would make it a topic of our family conversations.

There are some beautiful pearls of wisdom from our ancestors, and we make a point to highlight in particular those that consistently align with our family values. Two examples that my wife and I love and occasionally explained to our kids are "The Four Agreements from the Toltecs" and the "Mayan Greeting".

The four Toltec Agreements are: 1) Be Impeccable with Your Word, 2) Don't Take Anything Personally, 3) Don't Make Assumptions, 4) Always Do Your Best. As you read the rest of this book, you will see these concepts somehow reflected on how we talk to each other as a family, how we strive to solve conflicts, how we do everything we can to keep our promises. While we've seldom talked about the four agreements with our kids, more importantly, we believe in them and in a subtle way incorporated them into our family values and behaviors. If you want to learn more about this you can read the book **The Four Agreements: A Practical Guide to Personal Freedom (A Toltec Wisdom Book)** by Don Miguel Ruiz.

The Mayan Greeting is quite simple yet powerful. The Mayan words are "In Lak'ech, Hala Ken" which means "I am You, as You are Me". It can also be interpreted as "You are my other me. If I harm you, I harm myself. If I love and respect you, I love and respect myself ". This is more than a greeting. It is a moral code, a statement of unity and "oneness". It refers not only to humans, but also as a greeting and feeling of "oneness" with all life on earth. It has a drawing that represents two hands interlocking one at the top and the other one below.

This is in essence the Golden Rule of "Treat others as you want to be treated", or even better, the Platinum rule of "Treat others as they want to be treated" which is something we've reinforced with our kids since they were little.

Like these, there are many other examples of things we see, hear or learn from our Mexican ancestor cultures that are part of our lives today. Every time we say it and share it, we talk about it with pride and emotion, as this is something that is at the core of our roots and it is essential that we keep them alive.

Key Takeaways:

Honor and respect the wisdom of our ancestors. We all have them, our parents and grandparents are the key to learning about them. Be curious, ask questions, learn about the popular sayings and phrases that are part of our everyday life.

Be proud of your heritage and keep it alive in your family. Be intentional, say it and talk about it with your family.

Songs:

"Cielito Lindo" – Pablo Montero

"Mexico Lindo y Querido – En Vivo" – Alejandro Fernández

"Huapango Moncayo (1941)" – Alondra de la Parra, Philharmonic Orchestra of the Americas

Cafecitos con Mamá

"A coffee date with a good friend fills my cup
in more ways than one." – Siobhan Alvarez

Each parent can find their own way to communicate and connect with their kids. As I said in a previous chapter, mine is through doing something in particular, like playing sports, walking together, or doing other activities like assembling a puzzle or a Lego, or giving each kid a back/neck soft massage at bedtime. When I want to talk about something with my kids, I rarely say: "We need to talk", I would say instead: "Wanna go out for a walk, or to the gym?" or "Want a massage?", and since we start heading to the activity, we initiate our conversation about what I'd like to share or what I'd like to learn about them.

My wife also figured out a way to create a very special moment to connect on a regular basis with each of our kids. Since they were pre-teenagers, she invited them to have a weekly one-on-one date with her. When each of them was in their last year of high school, their schedules were very hectic, between friends, sports, social activities, school demands and preparation for college. Instead of stopping those weekly meetings, my wife told them this was something very important for her given they would go out to college the following year and she wanted to have those moments together before they left, and they needed to make it a priority in their schedule. She asked them to find a set day and time when they could do it, so it was planned and expected. Each of them made it a priority and my wife found with each one something they liked doing, and they would choose the place. For Andrea and Fernando, it was coffee, for Rodrigo it was Chick-fil-A. I think it is not really about the type of drink or the establishment where they go, but it does help them to do something they like to get started. If the activity itself is something they enjoy and the setting is conducive to opening up, it will provide the opportunity to connect and to focus on each other.

Having priority and the time to be together is half of the prize. The other half is what to do when you are together. My wife wisely used this time to get closer to them in every possible way, little by little finding ways to talk about everything that mattered. She would listen to whatever they wanted to share, their progress at school, gossip about silly things, ask about their friends and sure enough, open up about their love interests, talk about how they saw their life going to college, and anything they were struggling with. As they shared, she also shared stories about herself when she was their age and talked about the differences between generations and the similarities in values and things that truly matter.

Watching how my wife went about this, it reminded me of the story of **The Little Prince** when the little prince asked the fox what he needed to do to become friends, and the fox answered:

> *"You have to be very patient, first you'll sit down a little ways away from me, over there in the grass. I'll watch you out of the corner of my eye, and you won't say anything. Language is the source of misunderstandings. But day by day, you'll be able to sit a little closer..."* The next day the little prince returned. *"It would have been better to return at the same time,"* the fox said. *"For instance, if you come at four in the afternoon, I'll begin to be happy by three. The closer it gets to four, the happier I'll feel. By four I'll be happy! But if you come at any odd time, I'll never know when I should prepare my heart... There must be rites."*
>
> - **The Little Prince** by Antoine de Saint-Exupéry

The message here is to build trust, to consistently invest in a relationship and to genuinely show interest and care about someone. This applies to any environment and relationship. For instance, at work, as Human Resources leader, I've found that one of the most impactful ways to develop and retain talent is through frequent and meaningful one-to-one meetings between managers and their employees. These regular sessions provide a dedicated space for managers to frequently check in with each employee, talk about their overall wellbeing, listen to their concerns, provide and get feedback about their performance, do on-the-job training and coaching, co-create career development, and nurture a strong personal relationship, which ultimately leads to the employee feeling valued, cared for, and inspired to be fully engaged. In annual organizational culture surveys, there is a direct correlation with employee satisfaction, productivity and effectiveness with the frequency and quality of those one-to-one connections with their managers. All it takes is to have at least one high quality one-to-one session per month, consistently, to start seeing a meaningful difference. If I have to choose one activity that can significantly transform the organizational culture in a positive way, it is the implementation of regular one-to-one meetings between managers and their employees. In my view, it is one of the "crown-jewels" of human resource management in organizations.

And this has been true for our kids as well. Those weekly one-on-one sessions with my wife have done wonders in terms of their growth and development into adulthood. And have created such a strong connection, closeness and a ritual on the way they communicate on a regular basis to this day. Even though they now live in different places, they still have virtual "coffee dates" and whenever they are in town, or we visit them they can't wait to go out on a date together.

Ultimately the trick is very simple, it is about investing quality time, giving your undivided attention, listening, and doing it routinely, making it a ritual, so it becomes a natural and expected activity by both parties.

Key Takeaways:

It is paramount that each parent finds a way to communicate frequently one-on-one with each child to develop a personal relationship.

It can be done via sports, or having a coffee date, or doing something they like. The importance is that it is done regularly.

Song:

"I'll Be Here" – Colbie Caillat, Sheryl Crow

Promises Made-Promises Kept – Do What You Say

"People with good intentions make promises.
People with good character keep them." – Unknown

If there is one thing I can choose for my kids to say about me is that I always keep my promises. I've always believed that as a father, the most precious gift I could give them is the certainty that they can count on me when needed. When you see a daughter or a son tell someone else with absolute certainty that their father will be there or will do something because he promised you can feel the amount of trust built in that relationship based on love and personal accountability.

This is a huge responsibility that must not be taken lightly. If you promise to do a thousand things and only do a handful of things, your credibility is forever damaged. I see a promise as a very special gift, that works best when it is selflessly given, not when it is asked for or requested from someone, and it must be used wisely.

Having said that, no one is perfect (and I am the perfect example of not being perfect), and sometimes life happens and throws things entirely out of our control. In those few instances when the only option is to break a promise, it is truly about how you break it, so your word of honor keeps its value. In our busy lives with jobs, families, friends, and multiple activities that pull us in many directions, I've learned that making and keeping promises is all about focusing on what truly matters now and in the future.

Adding perspective to a decision can bring a lot of clarity when you need to decide between two seemingly impossible choices, in particular when it endangers keeping a promise made. As an example, if you learn last minute from your boss that you need to go to an event that conflicts with the promise you made to your little daughter to be at her theater play, you can add perspective to help in the decision by asking yourself: "In 10+ years from now, what would have mattered most? going to the business event or showing up for my daughter?" You can also ask yourself: "What would I like to have as a memory of today 10 years from now? Going to that meeting or going to my daughters' recital?" The answer becomes brutally clear. Life will present us with paradoxes and conflicting situations all the time. Knowing your values and being congruent with them in your actions and decisions demonstrates your character.

This works wonders for 95+% of all promises and events as it effectively helps you align your decision with your core values. For the very few conflicts that are entirely out of your control or the consequences now and in the future are too heavy so that it is truly inevitable your decision to break your promise, it is crucial to do it in a way that preserves the hearts of those involved.

For instance, a promise should never be broken by surprise, meaning the person finds out through someone else (a messenger) or after the fact. If you made a promise, you honor your commitment to go back to the person before whatever you promised takes place and communicate why you need to break the promise this time, owning your decision and explaining the facts that were beyond your control. And you do it the moment you realize you have made the decision to break the promise.

While there is no substitute for a promise not kept, you can establish a new commitment to fulfill your promise in the shortest time possible, the next time around, the next event. If there is no other event or another similar opportunity, you talk about the impact of breaking the promise, understanding the feelings of the person who was counting on your promise and own your decision to break it, with no excuses or blaming others for the circumstances as ultimately in the vast majority of cases (except when forces of nature or disasters happen unexpectedly) there is a chance for the person to choose to honor the promise or to break it.

Once the communication about breaking a promise is clear, there is no need to negotiate or bargain for a "make-up" or consolation prize. That is an easy way out that diffuses your accountability and appeases your conscience. The best thing you can do is to keep your promise next time to regain credibility. It is as simple as that.

When I say to use your promises wisely, I do not mean to avoid committing to doing things. On the contrary, I mean knowing your values and priorities well enough, so you can consciously commit to promise something that you know, no matter what, you will deliver.

I love to make promises and keeping them, and when I do, I truly enjoy the moment I get close to my wife and kids, or whomever I promised to deliver something, and with a hug, kiss or handshake, I can say the words: "Promise Made, Promise Kept".

Key Takeaways:

Your promise is your word of honor. Be consistent with your values to make decisions and commit to promise something.

If you make the decision to break a promise, own it, don't blame others or the circumstances, it is your decision to break it. Communicate timely, personally, with care and accountability to restore your credibility and trust.

Songs:

"One Call Away" – Charlie Puth

"Stand by Me" – Ben E. King

"Honey Do List", "Daddy Do List"

"The secret of your future
is hidden in your daily routine." – Mike Murdock

I am a believer in the power of habits and the power of focus. The power of habits can be summarized as: "Your destiny is your doing" much better explained by James Clear in his book called **Atomic Habits**: "All big things come from small beginnings. The seed of every habit is a single, tiny decision. But as that decision is repeated, a habit sprouts and grows stronger". This applies to all things we do in our lives, especially in our relationships. Said in other words by the great Greek philosopher Aristotle: "We are what we repeatedly do. Excellence, then, is not an act, but a habit". This is a reminder that our actions truly shape who we are and who we become.

The power of focus can be summarized as prioritizing those few things that truly matter, those "big rocks" that are the most important priorities in your life. I combined these two ideas: habits and focus, into my daily routine in a very simple visual reminder that I called my "Honey Do List" and "Daddy Do List". I created two post-it notes, one for each list and I wrote down the 5 simple habits that I decided to focus on as the things that matter most in my roles as a Husband and as a Father:

Honey Do List:
- Have time together as a couple weekly to nurture our relationship. No kids, no friends, just the two of us.
- Surprise her at least monthly.
- Support her goals and aspirations. Ask about them, show interest, tell her.
- Laugh and dance, as much as we can, as often as possible

- Romance! Romance! Romance! Love is a verb. Keep our romance alive with my actions, with small and big gestures, frequently.

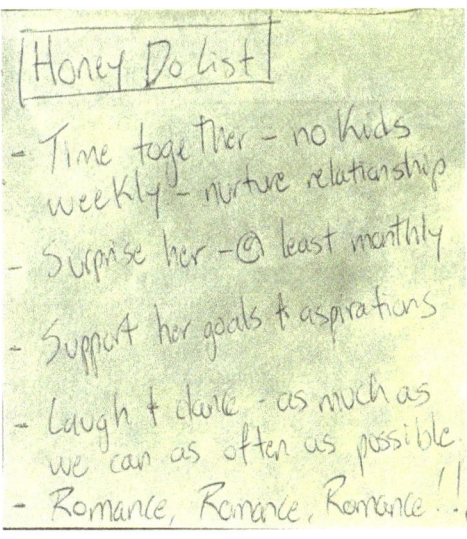

Daddy Do List:
- Find one thing each kid loves doing and do it with them often.
- Get to know their friends.
- Flex limits without compromising values.
- Set aside time to talk at bedtime.
- Be there for them, show up and be present at all significant events.

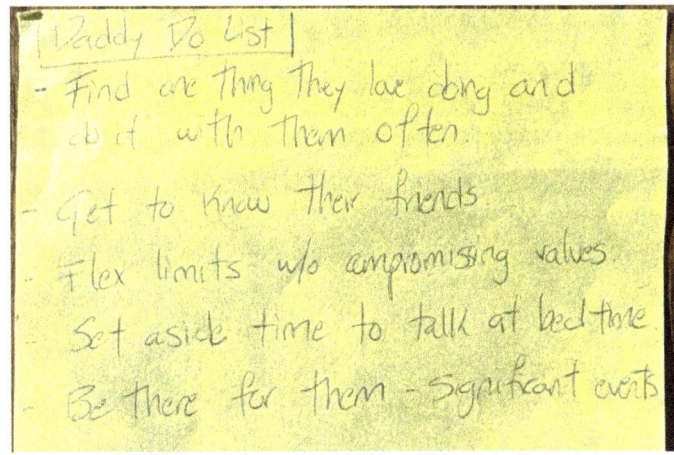

An Intentional Family's Love Story

I put these post-its in a place where I can see them every morning as I get ready for the day. It serves as a quick reminder, as my personal checklist for the day to nurture those precious relationships in my life. Having these habits identified is the first step, the hardest part is living them. I decided to put them into my calendar, for instance, scheduling weekly time with my wife on Wednesdays to go to the movies, I would set a reminder on a given day of the month to surprise her with an unexpected gift or doing something special for her (taking care of the kids, doing extra chores at home, bringing flowers for no reason, etc). I also do the same thing for my role as a father. I continuously think about what each one of our kids love doing: for my daughter it is all about music and dancing, for my son Fernando is a massage at night or going to the gym, going on a hike, and for my son Rodrigo is throwing a football together, playing basketball or watching superheroes movies. To this day, I make a point and plan to do these things whenever we are together. I review their interests routinely and as we age, I keep those things updated and continue taking the initiative to do those things together as frequently as possible.

I am not an expert in relationships, but I can tell you these things work. For instance, getting to know your kids' friends, showing interest in the people they want to hang out with, is a key to entering their world. It is about going beyond the superficial aspect of things like driving them around to do activities, or feeding them when they visit your home, or watching them do sports or play games. It means showing real interest in getting to know who they are, having a meaningful conversation with them, asking questions and listening to learn about their interests, their goals, and understanding how they relate to your kids as well, getting to know who they are without judging. Later in this book I dedicate an entire chapter where I explain this in greater detail.

Flexing limits without compromising values is the art of parenting. As kids grow, they want to explore more, do more, live more and that means testing the family boundaries. What they accepted yesterday without hesitation will be challenged tomorrow. Having a curfew hour to get home is a good example. The dialogue about a limit should not be constrained only to the rule to be enforced. It can be about the value that is beneath it, the reason behind the rule, and if the limit is to be flexible, the value still prevails. If the curfew is at 10 pm for a teenager, the core value behind is their wellbeing and safety. If the teenager asks to go beyond their curfew, the conversation needs to be about how to ensure their wellbeing and safety so instead of driving back alone, an adult or older sibling can drive with them and why that is necessary. The point is to talk about how to flex limits, always having in mind the core values behind each situation.

Setting aside time to talk at bedtime is one of the "crown jewels" of parenting at any age, from toddlers to teenagers to grown adult kids. Those last few minutes of the day, when they are about to go to sleep, open a communication channel like no other. It could be the peaceful setting, low lights, low noise, no distractions, and mind and body relaxation that creates a prime opportunity to share a few moments to share truly important things in a highly receptive manner. It could be as simple as asking about their day, having a ritual of gratitude of whatever they feel was positive in their day, praying together for something they care about, helping them download on you something that is stealing their peace and give them comfort, and share your encouragement, whatever wisdom or advice you can offer or simply just listen and help them fall asleep to rest and have renewed energies to tackle the problem next day around.

Being there for them at significant events is also a game changer. Whenever your kids have any kind of milestone, school event, hobbies or organized sports' important matches, teacher conferences, doctors' appointments, etc, knowing that they can count on their parents' support is key. When they turn around and see you there, something lights up that instinctively lets them know they are special, they are loved, they are the most important person in the world to you at that moment. That cannot be replaced. Showing up matters, at any and every age in their lives.

These things have worked for me, so I invite you to do your two or three post-its, define those 5 habits you want to focus on regularly on your most important relationships and bring them to life on a daily basis.

Key Takeaways:

Define the few important behaviors or habits that you can focus on in your most important relationships, with your spouse/life partner, your kids, or any loved ones.

Be selective, choose those 3 to 5 "big rocks" that you believe matter the most. Write them down and have them visible. Read them daily and put them into practice.

Songs:

"I'll Be There" – Mariah Carey

"Godspeed (Sweet Dreams)" – The Chicks

Solving Conflicts without Damaging Relationships

"The only way out is through." – Robert Frost

If there is one life-skill I can say I learned from my father, it is to solve conflicts without fighting. My parents have been married for nearly 60 years, and I have never seen my father raise his voice to my mother. I know they have had big disagreements, have been mad at each other, and had more than their fair share of reasons to fight.

In particular, I do recall seeing something my father did intentionally when tensions began to rise, as my mother would pick up the pace, and emotions got the best of her, I saw my father slow down, keep a low volume on his voice, pay more attention, listen actively and just take it all in. He did not withdraw, he stayed engaged and responded, but always in a calm and even manner. He would never swear, always being a gentleman, respectful in words and gestures and always found a way to keep the dialogue going.

My father's stoic example influenced in big part how I address conflicts in all my relationships and has reinforced my belief that it is possible to solve conflicts without damaging relationships. In my practice as human resources leader and coach of leaders, I have learned a few additional lessons which I believe make a difference when solving conflicts between two or more people:

- Listen first, paying attention (not thinking what to respond), so you can understand what the issue is.

- Before you react, ask questions to go deeper on the issue, to understand the behavior and why it is important to the other person.

- Face the issue together. Put it in front of both people. Visualize you both are in a rowboat with a hole. At the end, it truly does not matter which side of the boat the hole is, if you both don't find a solution, the boat will sink with both people on it.

- Always use respectful language. Keep your tone down, do not escalate things. This alone will go a long way.

- Don't just react to the conversation. Breathe, think, pause, so you can choose how you want to respond to solve the problem.

- The issue is either a behavior, an action or situation. It does not define who you are as a person. It is very different to say "I am upset because <u>you did</u>...." instead of saying "I am mad at you because <u>you are</u>....." Talk about the behavior, don't put a label on the person.

- Mean what you say. Mind your words and body language. What you say and how you say it can help move forward or make things way worse.

- Match your partner or other person's energy level. Pay attention to the emotion without judging. Don't defuse emotions (like making jokes if the other one is angry)

- Don't bail out – "whatever" is never a valid response. Own the situation, have a point of view, dialogue.

This is not easy work. It takes practice and willingness to let go of your ego and desire to "win" an argument. I learned this lesson from my father, who truly has no ego and only cares about what is best for the relationship. I learned from the master and tried to pass it on to my own family.

It is very important to learn how to do this in your own life, be it with a friend, boyfriend/girlfriend, life partner, and later on with your own kids. The first step is to role model with your actions, to demonstrate how you can solve conflicts without damaging relationships. I believe it is perfectly fine and formative for kids to witness conflicts between the parents and witness how they solve them, instead of sending them to their rooms immediately because of the fear of things escalating out of control. In a similar way that I believe it is perfectly fine and actually necessary for kids to witness their parents hugging and kissing. This teaches them something invaluable about how they want to emulate their parents' example into their own relationships in the future.

My wife and I have learned which are the core elements of our distinct personalities when it comes down to solving our own conflicts. When I do something that annoys her, I know that she needs to talk it through immediately, she needs to share what she feels at the moment. On my side, I need a bit of time to process things to sort my ideas and emotions before I talk things through. It has taken us a few "rounds" to learn this. When we both don't match our different levels of energy, we clash and it takes longer to solve our conflicts, but we ultimately do, following the principles outlined above. No matter how frustrated either of us might be, we do not let things escalate. We know our triggers and we know when we might need some time off. It is all about saying it, instead of assuming it.

As important as it is teaching our kids to solve their conflicts and for us adults role modeling how to solve conflicts with our spouse/life partner, it is important to solve any conflict when it is between your children and yourself directly. It is very important to realize that from a very young age, kids have a voice that needs to be heard and also that parents need to establish boundaries and teach their kids how to be accountable for the consequences of their actions, including when to assume self-accountability for doing something that could have hurt their relationship.

It is never too early or too late to learn how to solve conflicts in a constructive way and preserve the health of our relationships. Seek dialogue, inquire, and facilitate conversations to solve conflicts with their siblings and friends.

Key Takeaways:

Learning how to solve conflicts without damaging relationships is a fundamental skill we can pass on to our kids. It all starts with our example. Let the kids see how you solve conflicts with your spouse/life partner.

Focus on the behavior (what the person did and why it was important to you) and not who the person is (judgment). Put the problem in front of both, so it can be solved together.

Songs:

"Still into You" – Paramore

"You're Still the One" – Shania Twain

My Space, Your Space, Our Space

"There is no enjoying the possession of anything valuable unless one has someone to share it with." – Seneca

Learning to live together with someone can be quite an experience. Depending on your personality and habits, you could either not pay attention to it at all or it can be a central topic of conversation for a while. In my case, I am the second sibling of four and growing up I always shared a room with two brothers, then as I moved away from home, I lived with friends and then married. I have always shared space with someone else, so I learned a few things on how to make it work.

Have Your Space. No matter if it is big or small, I believe every household member or family member needs to have a space they call theirs. It could be just their bed and a chest, it could be an entire room and bathroom, it could be a studio, or any other spot in the house. This is a place where two things happen: 1) Each family member can express their own personality, be themselves, and 2) They can feel the ownership and responsibility to care for it.

Have Our Space. Aside from each family member having their own space, when there are kids in the family, I believe the parents need their own space and to truly keep it their own, grown-up space. In our case, we decided that our room was our space. While this might seem obvious, we have been very intentional about it. For instance, we only have pictures of my wife and me in this space, we don't have kids' pictures there, we don't have family photo albums or other things that are family related.

We also don't have kids' toys or clothes or anything that belongs to them. The rest of the house is filled with those things that are of course very important to our family life. But our room is our space, the place where we remind ourselves how we started, and who we are as a couple.

Of course, we enjoy being together in our room, cuddling with the kids in our bed, playing, talking, and living in the space as a family. This is not an area that is restricted, it just is a place that when the day ends, when we tidy it up, and everyone goes to their respective rooms, it goes back to being our space, our center, the beginning and the source where we feed and energize ourselves to carry on.

I know this might seem a bit extreme, and I can understand why someone might see it that way. But it works for us and let me illustrate it at two distinct stages of life:

The first one is in those early years when the kids are little, the house is a whirlwind of toys, diapers, clothes that keep changing sizes, gizmos and gadgets and all kinds of stuff that comes with their schooling and activities. These can literally be all over the house. As the day comes to an end and we finish the cleanup routine, it feels like an oasis to go into your adult room, just the two of us, with no signs of the little ones around as they are in their own space, with all those precious little things near them. It refreshes your mind and gives us the necessary break to recharge energy and start all over again the next day.

The second one is once they have grown and gone to college and beyond. At this stage, it makes even less sense to have all the remaining survivor objects, keepsakes, pictures and stuff stored in our bedroom. We have space aplenty, and we can be selective on the most precious things to preserve as they represent the highest sentimental value. At the same time, we want to keep those things away from our room, so they are not a constant 24/7 reminder that the kids are not there anymore.

We can certainly walk a bit more to see them where we decide to store them or display them in other rooms of the house.

Going to our room where we only see our things once again serves as a balm to our mind and to our heart. It gives us the necessary break to recharge energy and plan for the next time we are with our kids or simply to divert our minds from there and continue to plan other things we want to dedicate ourselves to.

Key Takeaways:

Allocate some space for each family member to entirely own, to customize to their own personality and expression.

Allocate some space for the couple alone, with no kids' stuff, make it your private "mind oasis" in your own home.

Song:

"Our House" - Madness

Spirituality in Action – Doing Service as Family

"I can't do all the good the world needs,
but the world needs all the good I can do." – Jana Stanfield

Every person and every family lives their own spiritual journey as they see fit. I respect all beliefs and ways of connecting with God or a higher being. Whatever the source of spiritual life, I believe it can come to life and bear fruits by serving others. The world sorely needs it and the most wonderful thing that happens is when you do it, you get so much more in return.

By doing acts of service, not only do you help someone in need, you also discover how to connect with other humans, to empathize with their situation, and you learn so much about yourself, your own beliefs, your paradigms and your own boundaries and limitations. You appreciate and have a higher sense of gratitude for your life and so much more. Doing this by yourself gives you all those wonderful learnings and doing it with others multiplies the effect and creates a wonderful bond of a loving community.

There are few things that can bring a family together as much as serving others in need does. The life lessons and the things you learn about your own family while serving others are invaluable. I have the privilege of seeing this with my family in many ways as we volunteered to help over the years. There was one time when we went on a mission trip to the outskirts of Mexico City during Easter week. Our kids were pre-teens then and the impact this had on them was almost indescribable. Seeing your kids interacting with other children that live in make-shift homes, with no floor, just dirt, with no possessions, and just enough food to get by, and watching your family caring for them, playing together, learning about their lives and understanding their reality for several days was a humbling and beautiful experience.

The importance of doing service as a family is the opportunity to get immersed in a worthwhile cause, to transform yourself into an agent of change for someone, to bring happiness, hope and alleviate the burden on others who need it, to show them the face of love through your actions. This is why doing service as a family lifts your spirits. It is not about the Instagram post, the # trend, the volunteer t-shirt or the school credits you may get. It is about making someone's life better, with love, and doing it as a family will pay back in so many ways beyond what anyone can think about.

Doing service as a family is also about building a stronger community. It is a responsibility that all families have to create the world we want to live in right where we live. It is not about giving what you don't use anymore or giving any spare cash to a homeless person as you walk on the street or giving something to those that are far away in another country that, while they very much need it, you may never see face-to-face. We all can do that, but more importantly, it is about engaging with those who live near and around you. That is the meaning of "love your neighbor", love all of your neighbors.

Recently I read **The Price of Humanity** by Amy Schiller who has a meaningful and refreshing approach to philanthropy. She defines it as: "Philanthropy should be a commitment to humanity's fullest expression, to build beautiful places for our communities to assert that everyone deserves beauty, social lives, art, opportunities for self-cultivation. As a way to use money to make people feel free". What a wonderful way to bring your family to engage in such aspirational purpose, to not only teach them to give what they don't need any more or spare a few coins for someone on the street, but rather to commit to a program that will break the cycle, to engage with the people behind it and get to see the impact on their lives through your actions.

If there is one thing I wish all families could do more is this, serving others together as a family. I plan to continue doing it, and I invite you to be intentional, get involved, find the time to do it and get your family excited about doing it together as often as possible.

Key Takeaways:

Doing community service as a family will give you much more than what you give. Beyond making a difference for others and improving your community prospects in life, it will strengthen your family love and bonds forever.

Be intentional, find opportunities regularly, engage with people near and around you, so you can see their faces and witness the impact of your family's actions in their lives.

Songs:

"Heal the World" – Michael Jackson

"Rise Up" – Andra Day

"Look For The Good" – Jason Mraz

"Shine Your Light" – Master KG, David Guetta, Akon

1 Million Kisses and "I Love You" and Counting

"Love is not something you find.
Love is something that finds you." – Loretta Young

Growing up, I learned a beautiful word in Mexico that my mother used all the time, the word "apapacho" which is from a Nahuatl Indigenous language origin and means to "hug with your soul". It is quickly learned by family members in Mexico and used as an unequivocal way to express love.

In our family we have many ways to "apapacharnos" ("hug with our souls"). Having moved across countries, we've traveled quite a bit, together as a family, back to visit our extended family and friends, and each family member has also travelled alone as they were growing up. Today, our kids have grown, they have moved out to college and all live in another state. The net result of the family lifestyle we have chosen is that we have grown accustomed to being separated in different places frequently. From a very early age, we began saying "I love you" every time we said goodbye, and that extended to every time we hung up the phone, or even every time we finished a text message. It has become part of our family love language.

I understand that in some cultures, saying the words "I love you" may seem to carry a lot of weight; for instance, you see in movies a couple that has been going out on a few dates and suddenly one says "I love you" and the situation gets awkward, the other person does not know how to respond, and overthinks their couple's entire relationship, with questions like "what did that mean?" , "why could I not say it back?", "if I say it now it will be odd", and all kinds of stressful situations ensue.

I believe that saying "I love you" should not be such a heavy deal. There are many layers of love all around. We say "I love you" at the end of a text or call, you can say "I love you" to a dear friend you have not seen for a while, because you loved reconnecting. And certainly, you can say "I love you" to someone you are dating without those fears of expressing it. Love is a choice, is an act and is a wonderful way to express to someone who is important in your life. That is all that it is. As we continue our journey as a family into this world, we will continue saying it, all the time, we are close to 1 million times, and counting...

Beyond the words, there are many other ways to "apapachar"; for instance, my wife and I have the ritual of not leaving home every day in the mornings without a goodbye kiss and not going to sleep without a goodnight kiss. And as a family we constantly practice our famous 20 second hugs. Somewhere I read that it has been scientifically studied that hugging for 20 seconds reduces the harmful effects of stress and is good for your heart. I can tell from experience that it does work. If you hold a hug for 20 seconds, you literally feel a wave of relaxation, inevitably you take a long deep breath, and instantly feel better (our son Rodrigo gets the trophy for the best 20 second bear hugs ever!).

My wife and I also regularly practice the 6 second kiss which has also been known to release oxytocin and helps create a stronger connection and bond with your partner. My wife and I are known for hugging in public as I do believe this type of wholesome PDA (Public Display of Affection) is perfectly fine. To see a couple hug or kiss, to see friends do the same, families and anyone expressing their feelings is absolutely fine. I believe it is much needed and can do a lot of good for our society.

Whatever is your way to express love, to "apapachar" and hug with your soul, do it with your family, any time, every time, and as much as possible. This gives your kids early on a sense of psychological safety, knowing and feeling regularly they are loved, and learning that love is something to be expressed, constantly, to say it, to receive it, and to make it part of their daily lives.

Key Takeaways:

Don't hesitate or overthink saying "I love you". Just do it with your family as often as possible.

Love is abundant. The more you give, the more you have to continue giving.

Song:

"I Love You" – Barney

The Christmas Gift You Need

*"The best of all gifts around any Christmas tree
is the presence of a happy family,
all wrapped up in each other."* – Burton Hills

I believe holidays of any faith-based denomination present a unique opportunity for families to reconnect with their roots and strengthen their bonds. The mere fact that people choose to be together, to travel great distances to reunite, and invest several days in the endeavor deserves respect and intentionality.

These are moments of connecting with all our extended family, bringing new members into the clan, sharing stories, learning more about where we come from, laughing, crying, dancing, praying, reflecting, bringing to life family traditions, and expressing our love for each other in many ways.

In our family we celebrate Christmas and along with the spiritual significance it represents, we have incorporated a few family traditions to celebrate our love. A simple one is wearing matching pajamas on Christmas day. Out of all the 365 days in a year, we all get to have a family sleepover wearing the same pajamas. It is a beautiful sight to wake up and see everyone wearing the same pajamas, sleeping late, waking up late and coming for breakfast wearing them. The fact that those pajamas might not be used much more after the holiday is not really important, but rather the purpose they serve in creating a shared memory; and if it comes accompanied by homemade pancakes eaten while wearing the pajamas together, it certainly makes the moment even more special.

Another very special tradition we have done for several years is what I called "you might not get the present you want; you get the present that I think you need". We started this with our kids to deemphasize the materialistic focus of how much money to spend on Christmas gifts. This is a family gift exchange where each member of the family would get something symbolic to other family members, many times coming from the "Below 5-dollar store" or similar bargain stores, or even better if it can be hand-made by themselves.

The idea is to find something that you think the other family member needs more of in their life and give it with a meaningful explanation. For example, if you feel someone needs more focus to achieve their goals, you could give a mini magnifying glass. Or if someone needs to relax more you could give them those cheap sunglasses.

One year, my wife was switching her career to a new field, so I gave her a small portable dry-erase board, symbolizing a blank canvas, where she would try new things, erase and do over as much as needed.

For my daughter Andrea, recently she has been working on launching a very unique project online, so she got a small ceramic paintable unicorn, as a symbol of the start-up she is creating in her very own way.

Our son Fernando had a very hectic year, so my wife gave him a desk mini-Zen garden kit with a little sand tray with tiny rocks and tools to rearrange as a symbol of balance and relaxation in his life.

In a recent year where we had significant change and family transitions, our son Rodrigo gave me a little desk ship enclosed in an acrylic box floating in a viscous ocean like fluid that creates the effect of an unsinkable ship as a reminder that as a family we can navigate any major change and storm if we stick together. When we do the gift exchange, we start with one family member who wants to go first, and give the presents one by one, allowing the recipient to open it and providing the explanation for each. Then the one who received the last gift will proceed and so on until all family members give away their gifts.

This is a truly wonderful family tradition as it requires each person to think about what every family member needs in their life, then find something that will symbolize it and give it with love and support for this to come true. Having all family members listen to what each one gives to others creates a sense of shared commitment to support it.

Key Takeaways:

Christmas is already a special time for everyone. Be intentional in discovering and bringing to life your family's rituals and traditions every year.

Songs:

"All I Want for Christmas is You" – Mariah Carey
"Esta Navidad" - Pandora

Keep Your Extended Family Close

"You don't choose your family.
They are God's gift to you,
as you are to them."- Desmond Tutu

Being a family that moved out of our country of origin, one of the biggest challenges is to keep our connections with our extended families, with grandparents, uncles, aunts, cousins and more. In our case, we left our country when the kids were very young (ages 4, 2 and newborn) and at a time when technology was not what it is today (no Facetime, no Zoom, no Instagram, no WhatsApp) so staying close and being part of our extended family's lives has been a challenge. Out of all the things you miss the most when you move abroad, not having the opportunity to have those frequent interactions with your extended family is certainly very high on the list.

We made a choice to be present as much as possible in the lives of our extended family and be intentional about our interactions to ensure those family roots nurtured our kids and us. It has not always been easy, but we are making it work. It takes planning, consistency and presence. Here I explain more about each:

The first one is planning. When you live in the same city as your extended family it is hard to make schedules work to see each other, you can imagine the added complexity when you live in different countries. We became very proactive, initiating conversations about planning for holidays, major events and milestones (significant birthdays, graduations, weddings, etc.) so we could find a way to be together in person as much as possible. As part of the planning, we make choices on how to have the means to be able to be with our families, we spend less in other areas so we can travel to be with them. When we can travel, we choose to stay a bit longer whenever we can to maximize the time we spend together. We believe that when there is a will, there is a way.

The second one is consistency. With young kids do not see their family members frequently, they can easily forget about them. The school schedule and duties, their friends, the after school activities and more, do not make it easy to have time to connect with extended family members. We became very intentional in sharing news with the grandparents about their grandkids' progress and milestones (losing teeth, learning to walk, riding bikes, significant school projects, hospital emergencies, etc). We err on the side of oversharing and over involving the families in our lives, always thinking "what would I share if we lived in the same place?" instead of thinking the opposite "they don't live here, so there is no need to bother them". When you want someone to be part of your life, you choose to make them part of your life every day. Of course, this has created tense moments, when family members can be "nosy" and inquire about that boyfriend in front of others, or pass judgment on something you did, or give unsolicited advice on something. But all those are part of what it means to have someone who cares about you, being interested in your life. And there are opportunities to learn how to relate to them, how to choose your response. What better way to "train" yourself on relationships than doing it with your family?

The last one is being present. When we have the opportunity to visit or our families visit us, we make a point to fully dedicate ourselves to being with the family, to making every visit truly special for us and for them. We plan activities to be together, we avoid as much as possible overlapping those trips with other things we want to do, and we fully join and participate in family traditions and special activities. We also plan for family members to come and visit us whenever possible to share important moments like graduations or holidays and dedicate ourselves to host them when they are around, so they get to see where we live and what we do on a daily basis.

These moments have created invaluable core memories for us and for our children and have created strong bonds with their cousins, uncles, aunts, grandparents that allow them now that they are adults, to continue sharing their lives.

In this complex and divided world, it is a blessing to have a loving extended family that cares about you, that advocates for you and is an unconditional resource and a cheerleader on your side. I've heard people say "you don't choose your family; you can choose your friends". I see it differently, we choose our family every day, we can choose to share our lives, to reach out, to stay in touch, to invite, to invest time together, and to continue having a meaningful and loving relationship for life.

Ultimately, however you treat your extended family will be how your kids and their partners in life will end up treating you when they fly away and form their own families with their own kids. I believe our example of wanting to stay close and nurture our relationship with both sides of our families will in return strengthen our own bonds as our families continue extending and expanding for life.

Key Takeaways:

Choose to stay close to your extended family. Have a plan, be consistent, be present.

Whatever you do with our extended family today is what your kids are learning about how to relate to you in the future as they form their own families.

Song:

"Father and Son" – Yusuf / Cat Stevens

Kor-Tim — Friends for Life

*"There are friends, there is family,
and then there are friends that become family."*- Unknown

One of the risks of moving as a family as much as we have done is to lose the opportunity to develop lifelong friends, those that you meet early in your life and grow up with. Usually, families tend to stay in one place, and go to the same schools for years, where kids have time to form deep relationships with other kids and share the same experiences as they grow. I do not think this is exclusive to any culture, I think it is human nature to socialize, to lay down roots, to form community with those around you. It is a way to ensure the survival of our species, by being surrounded by people you trust will be there for you when you need support, and also to enjoy their company, to celebrate important things, to have fun, to experience life together.

Fortunately, this is not something that only has to happen when you are a little kid. There are many examples of those life-long relationships being formed with college friends, or even later in life, with neighbors or other groups where you share significant interests. That was the case for my parents who formed a phenomenal friendship with a group of neighbors. They literally gathered in someone's house every Friday for more than 30 years! They traveled together with their entire families, and always found ways to have fun, celebrating holidays and milestones or just finding an excuse to get together any day of the week. As they got older, they continued being there for each other, through difficulties, through heartache, mourning losses together, and always staying close as much as possible. I found this admirable and as an example that I wished I could bring to my family life when I got married.

Once my wife and I started our journey moving around as a young family, we gravitated towards finding that sort of meaningful social connection wherever we were. We have been very fortunate to find it outside of our home country and have created very special bonds with several friends.

In Arizona we hit it off with a small group of international friends. Being our first move to the USA, we connected with other friends who lived nearby and were having the same experience. With friends from Germany, Mexico, Netherlands, England and a couple of local families from USA, we gathered regularly with our kids at the park, we played sand volleyball every Thursday, we bounced from house to house to celebrate holidays, milestones, birthdays and supported each other navigating our first experience in a foreign country.

In Brazil, we made a close group of friends from our kids' school. We literally sat together at the school orientation's day, and when we heard their Mexican accent, we connected instantly. This group became very special as we shared many interests and we all knew we were temporarily assigned in Brazil, so we decided to make the most of our time and explore the country together. We traveled as families, we talked about the culture, the differences, the rituals, and had a wonderful, shared experience. In Brazil there is a custom where kids call "Tío" (Uncle) and "Tía" (Aunt) the closest adult friends in your family. We all became "Tíos" of our kids and also became Godparents of some of them as well. Once our time was up to move out of Brazil, we knew that in one way or another, we would reunite in Mexico given our extended family presence in the country. At different times we returned to Mexico where we met again and continued our very close friendship that lasts to this day.

In Cincinnati we also found something very special. We reunited with several friends who many years ago started to work together in Mexico at the same company, and a few other new friends that also came to have an experience at the global headquarters of the company. As most of us were related to the company, and in some cases in the past we have worked together, it became usual to make references to our work life in our language, either as a relief of the daily stress or just as the inertia took the best of us in our communications, without even noticing. And one of the things that resulted from that was the name of our friends' group. There is an organizational term that in our company is used to describe a team that is at the center of a project, making things happen, who holds the responsibility for driving key initiatives, making critical decisions and ensuring the successful completion and delivery of results, it is called a "Core Team". Given we all were at work on different projects, associated with Core Teams, we all knew how important that is and as a joke, we named our group of friends the "Kor-Tim".

The group began more than 25 years ago in the unfinished basement of one of our friend's homes. This was the gathering place, where after our long day of work, any given weekend, we would drop by to connect, to talk, to laugh, to dance, and to form an incredible bond for life. From that basement, we evolved to rotate from house to house of each of the group members, bringing our kids all along, and bringing supplies in the form or a "paquete basico" (basic package) consisting of some finger food, the drinks we would consume, and something to share with the rest. Many of us had kids around the same ages, so they became very close friends, to the point they called themselves "cousins" at school which sometimes confused their friends and certainly it always helped them to feel they had more than enough "family" around if they ever needed support.

We traveled together to different places, made t-shirts for the group and became godfathers/godmothers of our kids as they grew up. In Mexican culture, you know that your friendship has attained another level when we call each other "Compita" (short nickname of "Compadre" that translates as "Godfather"). While not everyone was godfather or godmother to our kids, we all are "Compitas" to each other. We have been together at important events for our kids, at school performances, at graduations and certainly have been there for each other when someone had gone to the hospital or needed to be picked up from school for any special circumstances. We have become, by choice, our extended family abroad for the past 25 years.

As time has passed, most of the group have left the company and migrated outside of Cincinnati to pursue new jobs, the grown kids have moved out to go to college and gotten jobs as well. Work schedules and each of our own family life has pulled us in many different directions. But we stay close, we keep our Whatsapp chats alive and well, sharing all kinds of things as you can imagine, and making a point to stay in touch and seeing each other whenever possible.

Somewhere I read that having a group of close friends throughout life is significantly linked to improved well-being, increased life satisfaction and even longer life expectancy. I have indeed seen this in my parents, who are in their late-80s and regularly meet with their group of friends. I look forward to doing the same with all our dear friends and I hope that more families can experience the joy of having a similar group of friends for life.

Key Takeaways:

Having friends for life increases overall happiness and satisfaction, wellbeing and sense of belonging.

Having a group of families who are friends, both adults and kids, is priceless for their development. They can become your extended family wherever you are.

Songs:

"Sweet Arizona" – East Love

"Festa" – Ivete Sangalo

"Danza Kuduro" – Don Omar, Lucenzo

"La Vida es un Carnaval" – Celia Cruz

Wings

"The only way that we can live is if we grow,
The only way we can grow is if we change,
The only way we can change is if we learn,
The only way we can learn is if we are exposed,
And the only way that we are exposed is
if we throw ourselves into the open." - C. Joybell

To talk about wings is to be prepared both ways, for the kids to grow, to fully develop their own personalities, fine tune their skills and capabilities and make their first attempts to go out of the "nest" in a safe way, testing their ability to fly on their own.

For the parents, it is the stage to maximize their sharing of lessons and also to cherish the time being together, knowing that having kids means they are only borrowed and there is a countdown running that starts the moment they are born until they are ready to go out into the world on their own. From the moment they take their first baby steps, the distance they go apart from the parents little by little is longer and longer until they literally take off into their adult lives.

In the Roots section, I shared mostly rituals and experiences we had in those early years as a family. My hope is that a lot of them will be remembered as fond childhood memories, and my wish is that many will continue as cherished traditions.

In the Wings section, I share more of the character building and empowering concepts through interactions we had as our kids moved from childhood into their teenage years and up to their college stage. I talk about the things that I believe have been more formative for their skills to enable them to grow in autonomy and independence and be ready for their adult life.

These things include learning to cope with success and failure, their attitude towards what they can control and what they cannot, and self-management concepts regarding personal change and transitions. I also share insights on how to approach life as a wonderful miracle where magic can happen every day, but it won't happen if you don't do your best and make good choices and learn by doing the value of ownership and accountability by being responsible for making things happen.

I truly enjoyed writing about how important music and dance is not only as a family enjoyment activity, but as a form of personal expression and as a very important social skill, that allows us to connect with others, to celebrate life and form community.

I rediscovered wonderful treasures of self-reflection as I shine the light on our kids' soul-searching process to prepare for college and how to live life to the fullest, without the fear of missing out on what truly matters.

And I finish the Wings section on a very high note, by sharing our learnings and insights on accompanying their growth into the daunting process of finding careers they love and partners for life.

Song:

"Wind Beneath My Wings" – Bette Midler

Family Rocks – My Most Cherished Treasure

"Of all the rocks upon which we build our lives,
we are reminded today
that family is the most important"- Barack Obama

I believe that one of the most important gifts a father can give is to create opportunities for memorable family experiences and find ways to capture them and preserve them. In my view that is how rituals are born, and those rituals can become cherished traditions that transcend through generations.

We have a family ritual that started spontaneously almost 20 years ago during a family trip, and we have been doing it ever since. At the time because of my job, we lived in Brazil and went on a small vacation trip to the outskirts of the State of São Paulo, to a place named "Brotas". We stayed several days enjoying nature, hiking, horseback riding, beautiful waterfalls, excellent food and in the company of great friends. We stayed at a Fazenda (farm-like hotel) nested in nature. The entire trip was so beautiful that we did not want it to end. On the last day in the morning, we went as a family to have our last hike in nature and as we were heading back, the kids were tired and a bit down, so I came up with an activity. I asked them to go and find a special rock so we could take it home as a souvenir for the trip. I told them it had to be a very special rock, as it needed to be heart-shaped; to commemorate the love we had shared as family and with friends during this trip. I told our 3 kids to go on and find their rock and to bring it so we could select one to take home. They quickly ran and started finding rocks, sorting some out, throwing ones down and finally each made their own choice. I put all the rocks together side by side and we all voted for our favorite and one truly stood out, it was a perfect heart-shaped rock, so we selected that one and left the others behind. I wrote with a sharpie pen "Brotas", to remember the name of the place and added the date as well. Then I said that we were going to put it in a special place at home, in a vase, so we all can see it and remember the wonderful time we had as a family.

On our next family trip, on the last day we did the same thing, and the kids were beyond excited about repeating this ritual and that is how our wonderful collection of family rocks started as our treasure of all the meaningful experiences we've shared together.

From time to time, I take all the rocks out, put them in order, clean them and see our family journey. Some of the rocks were from a simple hike to a nearby park, others have been trips to foreign countries, or places where we've had significant family events, milestones, visiting our extended families in holidays and more. On every occasion, I do the same ritual at the end and get the family to find a heart-shaped rock to commemorate.

Now, almost two decades later, we have 240 rocks, each one representing a little piece of our family's loving history. We have a very large crystal bowl where all of them are preserved and at the center of our living room at home.

What began as a simple family activity, has transformed into a beautiful family tradition that grew in the heart of each family member. When our kids started traveling on their own, I was truly touched when they came back home and brought a rock from the place they visited to put into our family rock bowl. Now our kids are grown adults, and when we get together for a hike, or travel to any special place, I will ask on the last part of the gathering, "who is going to find the family rock?" and I can see their faces and body language turns them back into those little kids on that first trip to "Brotas" and they go on and help find the new family rock for us to keep.

When I look at the bowl full of heart-shaped rocks from so many places, it fills my heart with love of all those moments we lived together as a family, and it has become my most cherished treasure. It also reminds me that the best thing you can bring back from a trip does not cost you money. What you bring back are the experiences you shared with people and the new things you learned about others and about yourself. That is the best gift we've brought back with us.

It also reminds me that one of the most important investments a parent can make is in providing your kids with different experiences to broaden their minds, to expand their world. It does not always have to be expensive trips, it can be day trips in the same city to visit a museum, it can be going to listen to music at a park, or to be in contact with nature, or to visit friends and family. As long as you do it together, with the family, enjoying their time, and learning from each other, it will always be worthy of finding a heart-shaped rock to keep adding to your collection.

Key Takeaways:

The best investment a parent can make for their kids' growth is to provide opportunities to experience the world, to go outside of their comfort zone and meet with others who are different, to learn about humanity.

The most meaningful memory of a trip is not necessarily the location, the hotel or the landmark. It will always be the fact that the family were together, exploring, learning and having fun together. That is invaluable. Find a simple way to commemorate the trip and preserve the memory for the future.

Song:

"Heirlooms" – Amy Grant

Catch Them When They Fall **and** When They Succeed

"If you fall, I'll be there."- The floor

As many studies and science exist behind knowing how to be a parent, it still involves a big deal of trial and error, learning as we go, and with a lot of practice required, much like any good art. This becomes very real when it is about knowing when to catch your kids when they fall. From the moment they start walking, it becomes an ever-balancing act of watching them go, letting them get close to dangers, letting them take risks, letting them make those small decisions, and learning to live with the consequences as well. It goes from letting them have a bump on their head, or a scrape on their knee to coaching them to decide over their relationships, choosing their careers and so many things in between.

I've always been fascinated with how we are all born fearless and trusting. The image that best represents this in my mind is when a little kid jumps from the top of any place (playground, pool, stairs) into their parents' arms. At the moment of impulse, right before the jump, you see the kid extending arms wide open, with a big smile on their face, full of joy, taking that beautiful leap, trusting fully and with absolute certainty that their father or mother will catch them, and there is nothing to fear. That image to me represents how I want my kids to feel about every big decision and big moment in their lives.

As they grow up, it becomes more and more difficult to catch them physically, but we grow stronger catching them emotionally. And I believe that sometimes it is as important to catch them when they fall as it is to catch them when they succeed.

Catching them when they succeed means capturing those moments of greatness, when they worked hard to accomplish a goal, when they struggled and were able to come through. These moments should be surrounded with an atmosphere of personal victory, pretty much like an AGT (America's Got Talent) "Golden Buzzer" moment, when your kid gets an explosion of joy, with confetti all around and massive applause from everyone around. Then you can just cap it off with a heartfelt "I am proud of you", for your effort, for your dedication and perseverance to reach this achievement, without any judgment, or comparison, just a pure feeling of pride. I believe these moments serve as reminders of what they are capable of when they need it the most. Also catching them when they succeed is all about reminding them to stay humble, to not feed their ego and to remember that every personal victory is temporary and is all about their continuous learning and growth. What took you here might not take you where you want to go next. To take a moment to celebrate their hard work, to reflect on what made the achievement possible, to feel gratitude, to capture the learnings and to keep going. To make it come to life continuously, I believe that to capture when they succeed, can be supported with visual motivation reminders, to display in the house pictures of them doing something they love and they excel at, displaying their most important diplomas, significant achievements, to put them in their rooms, where they can see it to remind themselves of what they can do when they put their mind and heart into it.

Catching them when they fall requires even more care and compassion. It is paramount that parents let go of their own unreasonable expectations. The absolute worst phrase that a parent can use when a kid fails is "I am disappointed". Those words can destroy your kid's self-esteem and send a horrible message of "you are not enough through my eyes". Catching them when they fall needs to be free from any kind of judgment, it needs to be all about love, compassion and the opportunity to talk about learning from failure. Capturing those moments of trial and error, acknowledging the importance of having the courage to take worthwhile risks and feeling positive about the decision and willingness to experiment and try. It is also about reminding them of the importance of accountability, ownership and sportsmanship.

It is a wonderful opportunity for dialogue and reflection, listening and allowing for incubation and self-discovery. To act with a growth mindset and learn to pick themselves up and try again with new experiences on their shoulders and renewed energy as their parents remind them all that they are capable of accomplishing after seeing what they can do through the multiple times they were caught succeeding.

The beautiful thing about catching them when they fall and when they succeed is the strength of the bond it creates between parents and children. It is how you show with your words and actions that no matter what, you will be there, on their side, in their corner, in the stands and in their lives when they need it.

Key Takeaways:

It is as important to catch your kids when they succeed as it is to catch them when they fall. This will enable you to remind them all they are capable of doing when they need it the most, when they need that boost of energy to get going.

Being there for them when they fall and when they succeed is at the center of parenting. Be present, know their goals and aspirations and get involved as much as possible to be part of their journey.

Song:

"The Last One" – Maisie Peters

Do Your Best and Make Good Choices

"I am not a product of my circumstances;
I am a product of my decisions."- Stephen Covey

Over the years, I've had the opportunity to coach Senior Executives and leaders at all levels on how to achieve high performance and make sound business and organizational decisions. When I meet with them to help them prepare for an important meeting with their own bosses or to join the board of directors for an important project review, as we part ways, I find myself cheering them on and pretty much saying the two same things I frequently say to my kids when they were getting off the car or about to take the school bus in the mornings: "Do your best and make good choices".

Regardless of your age, education, experience, or occupation, one of the keys to happiness in life is about these two things. Why? because in life, those are the only things that you can really control, your behavior, your own actions and your decisions. All of the surrounding circumstances, context, influences, events, you cannot control. You can choose how to respond to them when they happen, that is all.

This is one of the most important lessons a father can teach their kids. I remember having this conversation with my three kids on numerous occasions. One analogy I would use is telling them to see their life as a Movie, or a Television Series. And I would ask the question, "in the TV series of your own life, what role would you like to be? an extra? a guest actor? a series regular? a supporting actor? or a protagonist, the main star?" Invariably the answer is "I want to be the protagonist!". And then I tell them they can be both the protagonist and the director of the movie, so they can choose what the protagonist does in every episode.

With this analogy, you can talk to kids, teenagers and adults about choosing the things they can control in any given situation. This is particularly helpful when they come home complaining about the teacher, their homework, their friends, their siblings, the weather, their clothes, and many other things, when they are acting as "victims" of all those circumstances, when their protagonist feels hopeless and becomes an "extra" who ends up usually being a victim in the series. To help them move from victim to protagonist there are a few powerful questions to ask: "What would you like to happen?", "What can you do about it?", and focus again on what they can control and take the lead role of their lives. Then follow up with "What are you choosing to do about it?"

Doing your best means bringing to life the best version of yourself today, and to be congruent with who you are and who you want to be. It is not only about making your best effort, or seeking the best possible grade, or seeking to win the first place in a sporting competition or overall trying to achieve perfection in all areas of their life. It is about growth, learning, accepting your opportunities, and knowing that it is ok not to be at 100% every day. When you bring your best version of yourself and give your maximum effort, somedays that would be 80% or 50% of what you have done other days and that is ok. As long as they come home knowing they brought their best today, they were their whole self, and learned what was different about that day, they will rest easy even if their best was not the same every day. Doing your best cannot be judged by other people's standards.

Growth is achieved not only talking about the result ("you got an A+ grade", or "you got the first place") and just saying "good job, I am proud of you", growth is achieved when you talk about how they brought their best self to play, how they focused on what they could control, how they responded to what they could not control, when they felt they were failing, what went wrong, how they learned and adjusted and how they want to incorporate those learnings for the future. Doing your best is not always a result, more often than not, it is just about being today a little better than you were yesterday. Also, it is not only self-centered, as most of the time doing your best means making someone's life a little better that day. Life is not a report card, it is about **doing our best** and **making good choices**, it is not about getting an academy award for the protagonist of our TV series at the end of the series, life is about helping our inner protagonist to choose to be happy in every episode.

Key Takeaways:

One of the most important lessons a parent can teach their kids is to focus on what they can control which comes down to two things:

1) What they choose to do (their decisions), and

2) Doing their best (their actions), and eliminate judgment, focusing on progress, not on perfection.

Song:

"Up, Up, Up" – Rose Falcon

Reading with Mami

"Reading is dreaming with open eyes."- Anissa Trisdianty

Learning how to read (the skill) is different from loving to read (the desire) and the determination to read (the habit). Like many other good habits, it all starts at home, following the example set by the parents. In our case, my wife awakened the love and passion to read, taught the skill, and nurtured the determination to do it in our family.

This is something she learned in her home, from her Father. To this day, I see my wife and her father talking about books, sharing recommendations, and continuing that special bond in their lives. She also actively engages in reading as a way to stay connected with her Mother and Sister and even her sisters in law. On several occasions she has organized a book club with them to select books of interest for all and regularly connect to talk about them and in the process, enjoy their company. She regularly belongs to other book clubs with friends wherever we have lived. In sum, my wife is truly a life-long reader who exemplifies not only how to bring the love of reading to her life, but to share with others with joy and make it something special in the way she relates to other people.

I had the privilege to witness and support how my wife introduced our kids to the love of reading. What naturally started as reading them short stories at bedtime evolved into teaching them how to read at home, placing names on sticky labels glued to everything around the house so they could read what it was (a couch, a chair, the table, etc). Then I saw how she got them started with small, illustrated books, then getting them interested in book collections for kids, filled with exciting adventures, then getting them excited about having their own library card and having special dates going to the public library or bookstore to select their books for the week, for a special trip, for the summer. The level of consistency and role modeling from my wife on the passion for reading is something I will always be grateful for. Our three kids not only acquired a love and passion for reading, but it also reflected positively in their overall level of communication, and their ability to express themselves, to write their thoughts and ideas.

Reading with Mom has given our kids powerful wings to explore their aspirations, and in the process, created wonderful moments of getting to know them, listening to their thoughts and reactions to a particular book, what they liked, what they did not like, what their opinion was about what the author was trying to convey, what was the point of the story. All of this develops, from a very early age, the skills of critical thinking and overall communication, so necessary to succeed in today's world.

Recently I read in Adam Grant's Hidden Potential about the importance of reading for a child and for society. In chapter seven, he talks about "Every Child Gets Ahead" where he shares the story of a global competition of countries regarding the effectiveness of their education systems. He features the story of Finland and how they went from being one of the lowest countries to be the best overall for multiple years in this global competition that included all the "first world countries". He shares details on how they transformed their education system to elevate the quality and as important as that, the happiness and enjoyment of students and everyone involved. It is truly an eye-opening chapter that I recommend reading. I believe that every school system should look at the lessons learned from Finland's case. The very first lesson that he shared from Kari Louhivuori who serves on Finland's Council for Creative Education is that reading is the basic skill for all subjects. Kari said to Adam: "If you don't have the motivation to read, you can't study any other subject. Cultivating the desire to read nourishes individual interests".

After reading this, I understood what a wonderful gift my wife had given to our kids. It reinforced the belief that the love of reading often begins at home. I read in Adam's book that schools started giving a free bag of books to every baby born in Finland. This helps to accomplish the very first step, which is to have access to books. You can do this via having them available at home or having the habit of getting them in the hands of the family by regularly taking the children to a library. The second step is to instill the joy of reading in kids by making books a part of their everyday lives. This involves talking about books frequently, at dinnertime, on car rides, visiting libraries together, and most importantly, having the kids watch the parents read.

Whatever we set the example of doing and where they see we value our time on an activity, they will want to participate and do as well. My wife instinctively fulfilled all of these steps and brought the entire family along in the journey. I am forever grateful to her for setting up our kids for success by creating in them the love of reading.

Key Takeaways:

Reading is the most important skill for our kids' learning ability. We have the privilege and opportunity to nurture the love of reading in our kids starting at home.

Make books available to your kids. Make reading an important part of everyday family life.
Set the example. Read, and read with your kids.

Song:

"Greatest Love of All" – Whitney Houston

From Doing Chores
to Developing Ownership and Accountability

"If you want your children to keep their feet on the ground, put some responsibility on their shoulders."- Abigail Van Buren

When you have more than one child, you get to see the "older sibling" effect. It is a role of assuming an innate responsibility to care for a little sibling. You don't have to explain much to your older child, you just need to say: "take care of your little brother" and they instinctively hold the hand of the little one and usher them around to do what they can to keep them safe. You can see their facial expressions change, they feel the responsibility, they talk to the little brother as if they were an adult, and most of the time, they do it gladly. Now, in a different context, if you ask the same older sibling to make their bed, or clean their closet, or help take the trash out, they complain, and ask you "why do I have to do this?" and after constant reminders, they end up doing it grudgingly.

What can make things more complex is when your kid believes the task at hand should be someone else's responsibility, or when they see there are no consequences if they don't do it at all, as ultimately, they realize that someone else will end up doing it for them anyway. This happens, for example, when you ask your kids to clean up their room and, if they end up not doing it, a parent, or domestic helper ends up doing it for them. How can we create more instances where our kids have that "older sibling", natural sense of responsibility? I believe it depends on two things: 1) Feeling they are doing something that they know is important for them and for their parents, and 2) Feeling trusted and empowered by you. I think these are two basic foundations of developing ownership and accountability and can be learned very early in life. But how to teach our kids to develop these behaviors?

In my work as a human resources leader, I have seen how powerful a very basic management principle is: "What is measured gets done and what is rewarded is repeated". This principle drives organizational behavior at work. That's where the concept of KPI's (Key Performance Indicators) to measure results came from and why they are used broadly on performance scorecards for employees at all levels. This is why employees have their personal responsibility charts that they review with their managers which determine their overall impact for a given period, typically a year, and in consequence will determine their pay and progression. If you want to change the culture, you need to change the leaders' and employees' behavior, and to do this, you need to change the rewards. This is human behavior in its most basic form, and it is learned at a very young age.

With our kids we started the idea of measuring and rewarding them when they could understand the basic concepts, around 3 years of age, and made it interactive and fun. We had a simple daily-habits poster hung up in their bedroom and every day we checked it with them, item by item and assigned stars to each item they performed. From that we moved to the idea of a weekly scorecard, with stars and giving them some basic rewards such as having a meal they liked, or going to a place they liked, playing with us more, or inviting a friend over. As their basic habits of hygiene, cleanliness, order and learning were established, we moved on to other simple chores, appropriate to their age.

From these basic behaviors, chores, and habits, you can move on to bigger rewards and projects where they can develop ownership and responsibility. Every family can set up the appropriate chores and rewards to incentivize learning and engagement. Many families use this concept to assign an "allowance" of money for kids to use as a reward to buy things they like. Whatever the formula for a family is, I strongly believe in the power of responsibility and rewards to drive the desired behaviors.

Also, it helps tremendously with the concept of delaying gratification that is so important in their development, especially in an era where kids learn from our environment that it is easy to get things instantly through technology given the all-encompassing access and real-time services that are designed to minimize the wait time for anything. You can talk to anyone and see them instantly through your iPhone. You can get any answer to any possible question instantly through searching on-line or even get an elaborate draft of what you want to know through artificial intelligence. You can purchase virtually anything through platforms like Amazon and get it shipped overnight. You can see real-time responses and reactions from thousands of people to things that are posted on-line. In a world like ours, teaching our kids to set their minds on a goal or reward their desire and work hard to obtain it, having to wait in the process is an invaluable lesson on resilience, perseverance and accountability.

It is also very important to help them feel empowered to act as they do the chores, not just to follow orders and do things because you say so. Think about when a kid is excited about a big school project, or when they have the idea to have a lemonade stand in their neighborhood or any similar situation. The way you help them will determine what they learn about developing ownership and accountability. It will feel different if you take over their project, buy the supplies, assemble the difficult parts, and stand next to them the entire time to ensure things go well, than letting them do most of the work, the way they envision it, and you just support and enable them on the things they cannot do (like driving a car, or paying at the store) and letting them feel the ownership, make their mistakes, and help them learn from them and keep trying until they succeed. In the same manner, delegating daily chores can be an opportunity to create empowerment and ownership. It feels different to shout the commands: "take the trash out" or "clean up your room" than taking the time to sit down to talk about why those tasks are important for the family (having a clean living environment, sharing the workload, educating the family about recycling, finding their own things in their room), explain the desired result (what good looks like, when the trash bins need to be out and how, what goes in their closet, drawers, bathroom, etc), demonstrate to them with your example (your own room, taking the trash out with them a few times), providing them the resources (trash bags, hampers for clothes, clean clothes and sheets), aligning how to review results and giving them recognition and feedback, so they understand the consequences or impact that not doing the task will have for the family and for them.

Doing this when they are little for those simple tasks, with consistency, can create the habit of responsibility and the onset of ownership and accountability. These will grow as they take bigger and more important tasks and serve them well when they become teenagers and want to work during their summertime and as they become adults to take full jobs, seeking to understand the importance of the work they do, and how they do it, so they feel empowered, taking ownership and pride for being accountable to deliver results.

To note, it is not always a straightforward process. As kids grow into their teenage years, it becomes more difficult to maintain a more formal structure of setting goals and a review process. Their eagerness to have autonomy and independence pushes back hard on anything that feels controlling or imposed. With our kids, we continued with the concept of responsibility and rewards, in a much lighter and interactive way, reinforcing important concepts on learning how to manage basic finances along the way.

Helping our kids to learn some basic financial literacy concepts and practices is one of the most important and oftentimes overlooked responsibilities of parenthood. By including this in a way that they could feel what it is like to earn their own money to do things they want to do, we found the necessary stimulus for them to stay engaged and willingly participate. Since they were little, we started to instill in them the behavior of saving a little money anytime they received a gift of cash, either as a gift from family members or from us or earning it through doing chores. My wife took each of our kids to the bank and opened a savings account in their name and we were consistently helping them go to the bank so they could make deposits of money whenever they had it. From learning how to use a savings account, later on we taught them how to use a checking account, how to make a basic budget of their expenses and the overall principles of living within their means, using money they already have, always paying their debts on time to avoid accruing interests and importantly, to have a mindset of abundance (vs. scarcity) when they think about money, to think about it positively, to attract it into their lives.

We linked the concepts of doing chores and acquiring more responsibilities with rewards that were meaningful to them according to their age. This is a very basic and powerful concept, to align in principle the things they want to achieve or get (rewards) and help them discover several ways to attain them (responsibilities), with our support following the principles of empowerment and delegation as I described above. We did not follow the scorecard concept during their teenage years, and it was fine. They had learned the basic concept when they were little, and our communication allowed us to align on what mattered most to them and we focused on how to enable, following the same principles.

This past year, life has given us the opportunity to retest this concept with other teenagers, more than 10 years after we did it with our youngest child when he was a teenager. We had two of our nephews, both 13 years of age, living with us for a year as they came to our home to study abroad. Given we did not have the privilege to educate them when they were little as we did with our kids, and we only had one year together, we decided to try the idea of a rewards chart almost from the start. We set a number of activities as opportunities for them to earn points, (volunteering, reading a full book, shoveling snow, cleaning the kitchen, getting an "A" on a subject they needed improvement, etc) where we assigned the higher point value to the things that matter most, and we defined possible rewards on things they would like to experience in their year with us (weekend trip to a nearby city, a day skiing, watching a sports game at the stadium) where we assigned a higher point value to those most aspirational or that involved more complex family planning. To note, we kept many rewards "free of points" like cultural things to do (go to a museum, go to the library, go to a cultural event) and we also made sure they knew they had activities they needed to do anyway and would not give them points (make their beds, clean their rooms). We used a similar chart to this one:

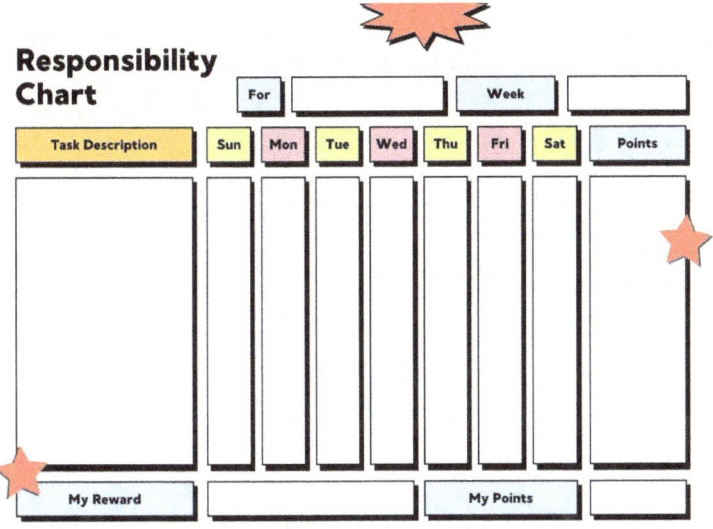

After several months using this concept, the results have been positive. We have seen them engage and work, each one in their own style, to earn the desired rewards. They have learned to wait and desire things they would usually have instant access to. A very insightful learning has been that aside from the activity or the reward is the fact that we have been talking about why they can't just get the reward immediately, and why they need to work for it when seemingly other kids where they come from might not need to do it. Seeing them engage in the dialogue, sometimes rejecting and not liking the idea, but with our consistency, coming back and participating, seeking to earn more points and seeing the rewards materialize because they've earned them, it has been a truly great experience for all that has reaffirmed the power of this concept.

Somewhere I read that there is a multi-generational study conducted by Harvard, that has been running for 85 years (and counting), where researchers evaluated the backgrounds of over 700 "high achievers" and found a strong connection between doing household chores and later professional success and more likely to be happier as adults. Some of the insights have to do with kids becoming less self-centered and developing a better work ethic. Kids who feel involved in shared responsibilities have a greater sense of self-worth and develop higher self-confidence. They become aware of the needs of other people around them and develop a sense of empathy and become more willing to help others.

Key Takeaways:

A great way to develop ownership and accountability in your kids is by teaching them to do chores since they are able to understand the concept and as early as possible

As kids grow, let them do the work (don't do it for them). You can use the 4 D's: Define the chore, Demonstrate it, Delegate it, Demand it.

What is measured gets done, what is rewarded is repeated. Whenever you can, make it explicit, make it visual, make it fun and engaging.

Song:

"Takin' Care of Business" – Bachman-Turner Overdrive

Mamá's "Polvitos Mágicos" ("Magic Dust")

*"All you need is faith, trust
and a little bit of pixie dust."* - Tinkerbell

In our complex world we are bombarded with so much information, tendencies, social media trends, social media influencers, all kinds of self-proclaimed prophets and experts, good and bad leaders, an exponential advancement of technology and science including the fast-paced awakening of artificial intelligence amongst so many other things. With all this feeding our brains 24/7, it becomes ever more challenging to discern what is true and how to form our own beliefs.

I believe parents can help their kids navigate this world by talking to them about the importance of caring about all of their well being areas: Physical, Mental, Emotional, Spiritual, and to learn how to choose the food that they need for each area and help them establish small but constant steps to develop positive habits on each one, for example: Physical = Exercise, Nutrition, Sleep; Mental = Reading, Study, Meditation; Emotional = Sharing, Listening, Positive Self-Talk, Journaling; Spiritual= Reflection, Praying, Gratitude, Service. Each one of these can be implemented starting with small regular routines, with constant support and of course a lot of reminders from the parents until the habit sticks.

There are two habits, easy and simple to implement, that I've seen have a very positive impact on our family as they can help to accelerate growth in every area and strengthen positive beliefs.

The first one is the <u>habit of positive self-talk</u>. Teaching your kids how to talk to themselves, to listen to their own messages, to break their own negative self-programming can be life changing. For example, just a change in words, instead of saying "I have to do my homework...", to say "I get to do my homework..." to see it as a privilege, as an opportunity to go to school and learn, helping them not to take it for granted, and to appreciate it. In the same light, instead of saying "I should do this..." to say "I can do this..." places the person in a position of choosing what to do vs. feeling it as an imposition or as something they do out of someone else's expectation. What we say influences how we feel and ultimately how we believe things are.

The second one is the <u>habit of gratitude</u>. My wife thrives practicing gratitude every day and has taught our family to do it in so many beautiful ways. She helps us to visualize and express daily gratitude as a magical and powerful way to attract abundance, joy and fulfillment into your life. Being grateful for who you are, for the things you have and for the things you want to receive and for who you want to become, as if you have already received it, as if you already have transformed yourself, attracts it into your life. You can do it at the beginning of the day, as you wake up, or at night, as you finish the day, you can make a short list, you can pray, you can write it down, take your pick.

And you can do the same thing with your kids. The key is to do it frequently, so it becomes a habit. As she taught us to do this, she would use a little hand gesture, like spreading "polvitos mágicos" ("magic dust") into the air and giving thanks to God for all those blessings in our lives. I feel joy when I see our grown kids now calling Mom and asking her to send them some "magic dust" for something important in their lives. My wife will talk them through how to do it via gratitude and will end up showing them the symbolic magic dust gesture via Facetime.

Whether you believe in actual magic is a personal choice, but we all can harness the power of gratitude into our lives with our thoughts and more importantly with our actions. And it certainly is a wonderful way to connect as a family, to reflect, to pray, to give thanks for our past, for our present and for our future together. And while we do it, like when we were all little kids, having a bit of pixie dust in our lives will brighten our day.

Key Takeaways:

The magic that we all seek in our lives is within our reach, in our habits, in our thoughts and in our actions. Ultimately, we are what we think of ourselves and what we do every day.

Teaching our kids how to talk to themselves with love and how to be grateful every day for who they are and what they can do with their lives are the keys for them to realize that the real power and magic is in them, they just need to choose it and behave as such.

Songs:

"Do You Believe in Magic?" - Aly & AJ

"Every Little Thing She Does Is Magic" – The Police

"You Can Do Magic" - America

Becoming Yourself
When Everything Around You Changes

"My identity is not my obstacle.
My identity is my superpower." – America Ferrara

Having the opportunity to move and live in different countries as a family has been an amazing experience, but it has not come without our share of challenges as a family and for each member. It can be intimidating to change school, city, country, language, culture, and leave behind your friends and extended family to start a new life elsewhere.

In all those moves, we learned a lot about changes and transitions and experimented with applying some of the same tools I used to manage organizational change along with some instinctive rituals to help us cope and adapt to our new lives. The first concept is to recognize that the change is an event, it can be chosen (you decide to move) or it can fall on your lap (your landlord decides to sell the house, and you must move); in any case, it has a clear start and end, one day you are in one place, the next day you are at another. The second concept is to recognize that the transition is a process, as it takes time to adapt to a new environment and, to move between the current state and the new state, we all go through three phases according to William Bridges' Transition Model in his book **Managing Transitions**: 1) Ending Phase, 2) Transition Phase, 3) New Beginning Phase. Here is how we lived these phases as a family:

The Ending: This phase is all about celebrating the closure of the current stage. It is crucial to have rituals to express our gratitude for all the experiences lived and to honor the wonderful relationships that exist in our lives. This is filled with farewells with friends and loved ones, visiting favorite places one more time, eating favorite food again, doing the things that might not be available where you go, and expressing all the love to all the people who are important in our lives. It is a combination of joy and sadness. A special quote that describes this phrase well goes: "Don't cry because it is over, smile because it happened" – Dr. Seuss.

To honor the ending phase, my wife created a very special ritual to say goodbye to our home, having a last meal there, once everything was packed and ready to go, and we would go room by room saying goodbye and expressing our gratitude to our home. We would remember the wonderful times we had there and thanked God for the opportunity to have a home like that. We also went and said goodbye to all the special places we loved. An important lesson learned as a family is that no matter where you go or if you ever return to the place, you will always have those memories and experiences as part of who you are now. The physical or emotional loss is there, but the experience and the memory are now part of the fabric of your identity and are not lost.

In this phase, it is very important not to bypass those rituals or try to ignore those feelings of loss. These must be honored and cherished. I remember one time when we had finished packing our home in Brazil and we had already moved to a hotel, getting ready to leave the country the next day. I was at the elevator with my two sons, they were 9 and 7 years old and my older son looked at me and said with his voice breaking "Dad, is it ok for me to cry because we are leaving?" and I told him "Yes, it is ok to feel sad and cry" while I pulled him closer to hug him. There was another man at the elevator and as the elevator door was opening, as he was about to step out, he turned back to us and said to us also with his voice breaking up, with teary eyes "it is always ok to cry, boy". This was a very sweet moment that reminded us how important it is to acknowledge those feelings of loss whenever they happen, and to never be ashamed of expressing your emotions.

The <u>Transition</u> Phase: Human beings are not appliances that can be unplugged from one place and plugged in another place and work instantly like nothing was different. Transitions take time and have a mix of letting go of the old and starting to explore the new. It can get messy. This is where you don't feel you belong anywhere. You have not yet adapted to where you are, and you miss a lot from where you came. Emotions run high, there is much more crying, complaining, denial and a lot of self-convincing that things will be alright. There are good and bad days, there are a lot of starts and stops, trial and error, back and forth, emotionally and in all aspects of your life.

This phase is all about progress, no matter how small it is. We tried many things at this stage, some things worked well, like my wife asking each kid on the first few days at the new place when returning from school to write on a post it one thing they liked about their day; I gave them the goal to make one friend the next day and celebrating those baby steps. It involved reaching out to other parents to invite their kids to a birthday party, showing up at school frequently to see how things were going and volunteering for field trips, going for lunches and checking constantly to anticipate issues. We had our share of sadness, a little bit of bullying and even the need to intervene at some schools to ensure there was enough attention paid to the needs of our kids. Transitions can take a long time, particularly when things don't work as expected. Asking for help and closely monitoring those first weeks makes a huge difference.

The <u>New Beginnings</u>: This phase is all about exploring possibilities and capturing early wins. I call this the phase of "finding the spark" that will light the positive fire and create momentum towards the new life. Sometimes it comes in the form of a new friendship, it could be a boy/girl that they like that smiles back, or it can be when they decide to take a risk to do something new, something different and succeed, changing their look, or learning something exciting. When they find that spark, you see it in their eyes, you hear it in their voice, their excitement is unmistakable, and you run with it. You find opportunities to do more of it, celebrate it, make it grow. In many ways, this becomes a discovery of new possibilities for them. Our daughter discovered her talent for music, learning how to play guitar in one of our moves and her love of performing in another. Our middle son discovered his talent for art and writing by visiting museums and learning from a great teacher and found joy playing individual sports like tennis and running. Our youngest son discovered his passion for drawing, for playing soccer and team sports to connect with friends. All those skills not only helped them transition through a specific change, they are now an integral part of their identity.

The three phases show each family member a lot about who they are and who they want to become. The ending phase celebrates your history, where you come from, those roots that you choose to bring forward into your life. The transition phase tests your resiliency, it is when you begin expanding your wings, taking risks, falling sometimes, soaring other times, it hones your adaptability and strengthens your will power. And the new beginning phase serves as a catalyst to reshape your identity, creating the foundations for those lifetime bonds, bringing all the learnings, all the experiences and all possibilities together.

Key Takeaways:

Growing up is a constant experience in change and transitions. Learning a bit on how the three phases of changes work (ending, transition, and new beginning) can help parents understand and support their kids throughout the different stages in life.

Discovering family rituals in each phase of change are great opportunities to help the family members not only to move forward but to have cherished memories forever.

Songs:

"Unwritten" – Natasha Bedingfield
"Hold On" – Wilson Phillips

Social Interactions –
Grow Their Own Voice and Self-Confidence

"Children are like wet cement:
whatever falls on them makes an impression." – Haim Ginott

My parents have always been very sociable, frequently in contact with people, be it family, friends, their community at church, and the different groups of parents at all the schools we attended. Both are past 85 years old and keep doing so, despite the limitations that come with old age. They are great at staying close to their lifelong friends, and are open to making new friends, even now. Perhaps this is one of the main reasons why they continue enjoying longevity, as having an active social life plays a key role in our mental wellbeing.

As far as I can remember, the home where I grew up was a place to bring people, to celebrate family and friendship. My parents had a regular group of friends that met every Friday evening for more than 30 years. Many of those gatherings were at our home and from a very young age, my parents somehow made us part of their friends' interactions. We were called to greet and say hi to every adult, one by one, shaking their hands or with a side hug/kiss, and were invited to stay there for a little while to interact with their friends and share a bit about our lives. When we were kids, after those moments of early social interaction, we were sent upstairs, and I remember sitting down at the stair steps with my siblings, listening to their laughs, dances and fun. As we were growing up, we were invited not only to say hello and be there for a few minutes, but to be part of their celebrations, we met their kids and ended up traveling together and became good friends with some of them.

Those early social interactions made an impression on me. As a kid, they helped me to take my first steps communicating with adults, to gain confidence in a safe space, where I felt loved and cared for. Their questions about what I liked at school, sports, my friends, and other topics were questions about me, where all the answers were entirely up to me, there was no right or wrong, I did not have to study or pretend so I felt at ease responding and interacting with them.

As I grew up, I realized how formative it can be for kids to be listened to, even when they are very little, to truly pay attention to what they say, to help them find their voice, to express their thoughts and feelings, and avoid as parents to become their interpreters in social situations, either guessing what they want to say, or telling them what the parents think they should say in front of other adults.

We all can learn not to be afraid or discouraged because of long silent moments, or pauses, while kids (and sometimes adults) collect their thoughts. We can avoid the temptation to blurt things out just to keep the conversation flowing, or to hold the attention span of others. That is not the goal. It truly is about helping our kids to find their inner voice, to listen to it, to practice saying what they want, what they feel, what they mean. Their thoughts and words might not come out well articulated, they might fumble a few times, say something weird, or might shut down after their first try. That is when we can support them instead of putting more pressure on them. We can be patient, ask them to take their time, or to find another way to express what they want to say, perhaps to draw it, to sing it, to dance it, or just to think about it and talk later when they are ready. It is all about building their confidence and that happens with patience, practice and support.

As my wife and I had our own kids, we've consciously talked about this and purposely have put it into practice. We've also brought our kids to be part of our social interactions, with other adults, with all our friends. We've asked them to say hello to every single adult in the room, to shake their hands firmly, to look at them in the eyes, to not only stay there, but to interact, to share in their own words what they think, and to inquire back, to ask them about their lives, to show interest in the other person. And after many of those social interactions, we've talked together about who they met, what they learned, and how they felt. While it has not always been a smooth ride, we can tell it has helped them develop their own social voice and build some foundational social interaction skills.

Beyond our own friends, we instilled in them the expectation to interact with other adults in their lives, the parents of their friends, and as they grew into teenagers and turned into young adults, to deliberately interact with the parents of the people they went out with on a date. If they are out to pick up a date, they need to park the car, go to the house, meet and greet the parents and have a conversation, sharing about themselves, asking questions and showing interest and care about others. I believe it is crucial for our kids to learn how to socialize with others, to learn how to relate to the generations above, to respect them, and it is up to the adults to show them the way, to invite them in, to open the door and enjoy those interactions. It is never too late to try this on, in your next opportunity, invite the kids to stay with a purpose, and facilitate the interaction in a way that builds their self-confidence.

Key Takeaways:

Social gatherings of adult friends are great opportunities to "train" our kids to develop social interaction skills from a very young age.

Empower and enable them to find their own voice, express their thoughts with their own words, be patient, don't mind the silence, and support them along the way.

Song:
"Brave" – Sara Bareiles

Dance Like Everyone Is Watching!

"To dance is to be out of yourself.
Larger, more beautiful, more powerful.
This is power, it is glory on earth,
and it is yours for the taking." – Agnes de Mille

For many people, dancing is just a social convention, a ritual that comes associated with events and celebrations such as graduations, weddings and other kinds of parties. For others, dancing feels like something you must endure, it is something you need to learn to be able to not make a fool of yourself in public. For others it can be a form of exercise, to get in shape, and for those who are very disciplined and talented, dancing becomes their purpose and can become their way of living. I'm sure there are studies that can correlate the benefits of dancing for our wellbeing. There is a social component, as any time you dance with others, you communicate and if you do it regularly with friends, you create community. There is a mental component, the smiles, laughs, the stimulation of your senses, following the tunes, singing the songs, and the coordination to move along with the rhythm. There is a physical component, as you move pretty much your entire body, your muscles, you stretch, you accelerate your heartbeat, you breathe deeper to shout, to sing, and increase your stamina to stay on the dance floor. And there is an emotional component as dancing with a partner can evoke deeper feelings, you connect physically, synchronize your moves and experience being present together.

To me, dancing has been a very special part of who I am. Just like the **Billy Elliot** movie, when he was auditioning to join the ballet school and one of the teachers asked: "what does it feel like when you are dancing?" and he said: "I don't know, once I get going, I forget everything, I can feel a change in my whole body, like there is fire in my body, I'm just there, flying, like a bird...like electricity". That pretty much sums up how I feel about dancing. As long as I can remember, when there is music, I'll be out there, feeling the music and enjoying dancing, most of the time with others, and on many occasions, just by myself.

Growing up, I loved watching my parents dancing, in particular rock and roll. The way they were synchronized, the spins, their smiles, it was all perfectly choreographed. As a little boy, my father once told me "Those who dance, get the girl" and he taught me the basics to dance as a couple. I have early memories of my parents and my siblings learning together how to dance at home, on any given weekend. That became an image of what I wanted to do with my own kids in the future.

I have been very fortunate to fall in love with someone who also likes to dance. We both enjoy dancing together and have gifted our kids with the love for music and joy for dancing. Since they were babies, we held them up, danced together as family and passed on to them their grandparents' teachings. Our three kids have learned all the fundamentals of dancing in couples and have developed their very own personal style on the dance floor. It is a beautiful thing to see how their different personalities come to life in their moves and how they relate to others on the dance floor. There are few things in life that I enjoy as much as dancing with my adult kids now.

Dancing for our family has become one of our love languages. There is something really special that happens when you truly dance with your loved ones, and let go, jump, choreograph steps together, show some of your best moves, learn new moves from your kids and just be fully present. The wonderful thing about dancing is that it involves most of your senses. You cannot be dancing and checking your phone or even having a conversation; if you let yourself be immersed in the music, feeling the rhythm, and engaging with those around you, dancing becomes a true form of human connection that can create everlasting memories and nurture those relationships' bonds with those you care the most for.

My wish is for our kids to extend our dancing love language to their own families. My invitation is for every family to experience the joy and bonding that comes with dancing together. Do not worry about skill or about what others may think as you let yourself go. All it takes is to feel the music and express whatever comes naturally to you at the moment, close your eyes, listen to the rhythm and let your body flow, do not think, just do it.

Key Takeaways:

Dancing is one of the most complete and beautiful forms of expression and human connection.

Enjoy dancing regardless of the skill level and practice it together as a family as often as possible.

Songs:

"La Ventanita" - Garibaldi

"Te Contarán" – Juan Luis Guerra

"Yo No Sé Mañana" – Luis Enrique

"Can't Stop This Feeling" – Justin Timberlake

"Dancing with Myself" – Billy Idol

"Footloose" – Kenny Loggins

"Arerê – Ao Vivo" – Banda Eva

College Essays – A Jewel of Self-Discovery

"It's on the strength
of observation and reflection that one finds a way.
So, we must dig and delve unceasingly." – Claude Monet

Like the African proverb says, "It takes a village to raise a child", this certainly becomes very real when your kids decide to go to college and it is time to prepare for it. The process, at least in the USA, is certainly complex, and it becomes an important family matter in particular the last couple of years of high school education. That is when kids and parents are very aware of the impact of their academic grades, the extracurricular and leadership development activities, community service, sports, student associations, clubs, and other things that can play a factor on the overall strength of the submission packet to increase the chances of being admitted at the preferred institution and the possibility to receive financial support.

It feels like an obstacle race, or I should better say it feels like a "Jumanji" adventure. It involves working hard on all subjects to get good enough grades, and in particular on those very hard to earn AP (advanced placement) grades. It also involves preparing and taking several rounds of standardized tests to improve their scores, securing letters of recommendation from teachers, taking long road trips to visit schools, the not so easy decision on segmentation of choices between in-state, out-of-state, dream college, safety college, campus vibe, city vibe, rooming options, roommates' selection, to declare a major of choice or be undecided, and so many things in between.

As a parent, you have three choices on how to live this process: 1) Enjoy it, 2) Suffer it, or 3) Abdicate it. Whatever the family situation, I strongly recommend choosing to enjoy it, no matter how daunting, intense or cumbersome the entire process may seem. Like other unique moments in your family life, this experience most likely will only happen once for each kid, and how you choose to be involved and how you choose to behave and respond, will mark your relationship in a big way. Having done it three times with our kids, I can tell it is a fascinating family experience that has left unforgettable core memories for us to cherish forever.

One of the most beautiful memories has been witnessing how each kid prepared their own college essays. I believe these are pure treasures. Most universities require that all applicants write around 500 words on relevant subjects like: "Why This College?", "Why Your Major?", "Describe a significant challenge you overcame," "Reflect on a time you questioned a belief," "Discuss a topic that captivates you or deeply interests you," "Describe a person you admire"

Nowadays, kids have the temptation to use artificial intelligence (AI) tools to substantially help to generate their college essays. Besides the fact that colleges can use their own AI tools as well to detect essays that used AI, there are the issues of questionable integrity and lack of authenticity. The sole purpose of the essay is to see the ability to express in words how the applicant thinks and their values and beliefs, and that cannot be done through AI tools. Beyond that, there is no AI tool that can know the personal story and growth experiences of the applicant. This is why I believe college essays are such a wonderful opportunity for self-reflection and personal expression.

As part of the essay, applicants end up sharing a great deal about their own story and their journey in life so far. They reflect on their challenges, how they overcome obstacles, and while doing so, most inevitably, end up with a strong sense of gratitude for who they are and who they want to become, which manifests itself as they write up their thoughts and beliefs.

Writing a college essay can also be seen as a "rite of passage", as it marks a symbolic transition in their lives. As they deeply reflect on their personal experiences and aspirations in life, they take a big step towards adulthood. The fact that, like your own kids, most high school students, in particular their close friends, go through the same process of self-discovery and deep self-reflection at the same time creates a beautiful opportunity to have a shared understanding of their values, goals, identity, and learn more from each other about who they are and who they want to become.

For our kids, we had an opportunity to learn beautiful things about how they saw their upbringing and what experiences forged their identity. They all wrote transformative essays with insights that are worth sharing broadly.

Our oldest daughter Andrea, wrote about how she discovered the importance of human connection in a world of extremes and contradictions. She talked about how she stepped into reality through a mission trip where her "little glass box" where she lived sheltered was shattered into experiencing another drastically different reality. This experience transformed her awareness, empathy and gratitude as she realized that everyone, regardless of circumstantial contrasts and contradictions, is the same in the things that matter. Here is the full essay:

Andrea León-Ramos
Honors Essay

We live in a world of contradictions. A world characterized by its ability to have extremes. This ability is maintained by what I like to call, "little glass boxes". Every culture has them, and they can be helpful in keeping traditions and beliefs strong, in creating unity in community and preserving innocence. These little glass boxes serve as protection from the extremes we do not want to deal with, they create comfort zones and limits. Through their clear walls, we can see what is happening elsewhere, but have that safe distance that prevents our sensory understanding of it. People often say that we live in our own personal "bubbles" in trying to convey this idea, but in my opinion that term is incorrect; bubbles are too easy to pop, too easy to break out of. Comfort zones are not. Many will live in their glass cases forever, content in their innocence and ultimately, in their ignorance. Many others, however, choose to step outside those four walls and into humanity.

My glass walls were shattered on a mission trip in 2010. My church was organizing a weeklong trip to the outskirts of Mexico City, to help a small community. The whole week would be spent with them from 7am to as late as 10 pm, helping with any and all tasks they required. I'll never forget the moment I stepped into the first house to meet the first family, for it was then that the first cracks began to form in my little glass box. We walked up to a small, one-story adobe house painted a light blue, its weathered paint peeling. The priest knocked on the door, and a boy around ten years old (the age of my youngest brother) opened the door. He welcomed us indoors with a smile that radiated admiration and joy, and introduced us to the other five members in his family that shared that small single room house. An excited chatter bounced off the walls, welcoming hugs and kisses from every member in that family, neighbors called over for introductions. There was no physical contrast between that little home and its surroundings; the floor both inside and outside was the earthy ground, the air was just as hot and stifling inside and out, the animals ran about freely in both, however the atmosphere inside that little home was one of humility, openness and instant acceptance which created a beautiful distinction between that little home and its surroundings.

During that week, I felt an immense change in me. Thinking

back, I often try to pinpoint the source of my transformation. Maybe it came from walking door to door and hearing every person's story, hearing their own battle, which put my own struggles into perspective. Maybe it came from receiving lunch from a family that struggled to put a single meal on their own table. Maybe it came from meeting a 78-year-old woman who slept on a rock every night, dreaming of mattresses. Maybe it came from seeing my brothers confide in and play with boys and girls with nothing more than a soccer ball, dust hills and their imaginations. Maybe my walls came down when children gathered around my guitar on a sweltering hot day and sang with me, clapping and dancing and feeling, forgetting the fact that we were two extremes and focusing on the fact that we were singing the same songs. It was in the emotions that played on everyone's faces, because in seeing their sadness, joy, fear, determination, frustration and gratitude, I saw my own emotions reflected back at me. A difference in situation, a perfectly similar humanity.

My change came from realizing that everybody, regardless of their circumstantial contrast and contradictions, is the same in the things that matter. And although the whole community said more "thank you's" than I can count, and expressed their gratitude in numerous ways, I will never be able to repay them for the change they brought in me; for the shattering of my little glass box.

More than 10 years later, I've seen how that seed that was planted in her soul has grown as she has become an artist and educator who advocates for social equality and activism for kids.

Our middle son Fernando, wrote about discovering his roots amidst the constant moving of countries, cities and houses that characterized his upbringing. These experiences transformed his personality and character, by acquiring the skill of resilience and adaptability, and embracing new beginnings and departures as part of life. His discovery of having the strength and resiliency of a "weed" constantly growing roots being nurtured by new soil and being pulled away and leaving part of himself behind is a beautiful reflection of how he has formed his personality, while knowing his home and roots are wherever he is at the moment. Here is the full essay:

Fernando León-Ramos
College Essay

7:20 on a Monday morning. I sat on my stool behind an untouched lump of clay, dumbfounded. A wave of anxiety washed over me as my eyes darted around the room. Everywhere I looked, fingers danced through clay forming intricate doors, roofs, and windows; but not mine. My fingers were stuck tracing the same sentence over and over again.

"Create a sculpture that represents your home."

I repeated it under my breath. "Home"— a word that I had called out thousands of times. After track meets and art classes, nights out with friends, and trips abroad, I always returned home; but home wasn't always the same place.

Wrapped in a hospital blanket in my mother's arms, I came home for the first time to a two-room apartment in Queretaro; its walls watched curiosity guide me to hidden cupboards and dark corners.

Leaping across the pebble path that burnt my toes, I ran home to the cream-colored house in Arizona: a house where kids ate applesauce and escaped the heat in a backyard pool.

Anticipating the ding of the 14th floor, I rode the elevator home to the apartment in Brazil: a maze of hallways with a balcony where I stood on my tiptoes to marvel at the city around me.

Sitting cross-legged in a school bus, I stared out the window the entire ride home to the suburban house in Ohio. The brick walls and pointed roof matched the pattern of the neighborhood, and the creek outback transformed into my imaginary world.

Stuck in the eternal traffic of cars and blaring horns, I waited on the way home to the modern house in Mexico City. A cube of frigid tile, metal, and glass formed the only place where I felt safe from the dangers of the metropolis.

And the list went on, with days at la casa de los abuelos, weeks in hotel rooms, and months in temporary living complexes. Home wasn't a single place. Home was in three countries and seven cities, which made it feel like home was nowhere at all.

"Acuérdate Fer, tu hogar es donde están tus raíces".

My parents' voices echoed in my head. Every time my dad's job got us to cram our lives into a moving truck, I was told that home is where my roots are—an analogy that was meant to reassure me, but instead made me feel like a garden weed.

Yes, a garden weed.

I constantly struggled to claim my spot in communities where everyone else had grown up together; communities where everyone's roots were intertwined deep beneath the surface. Then, when I finally started to feel like a new place was my home, my roots were yanked out from beneath me and planted in foreign soil.

At first glance, being a weed was unbearable. Hours of gardening with my mom had taught me that weeds are annoying and invasive—they held their ground whenever I fought to unearth them, and always managed to leave pieces of themselves in the soil. Only a few days later, they'd have sprouted up again—but then, I realized that those same irksome qualities of weeds were some of the best qualities in me. Weeds are resilient and adaptable; they find ways to thrive wherever life puts them. Just like a weed, I left parts of me in every place I lived, and absorbed nutrients from every soil. In each location, my roots grew stronger with distinct cultures and experiences.

I made connections around the world and I made the world my home.

8:20 on a Friday morning. I sat on my stool behind my finished sculpture with confidence. The clay figure was simple—a small house propped on a globe—but it was symbolic. Around me, my classmates titled their art with street names and zip codes, but not me.

Name: Fernando León-Ramos
Class: Sculpture
Title: Scattered Roots: Home is Everywhere

Now, many years after finishing college, I see his hunger to travel, his desire to meet and experience new cultures, and be a citizen of the world, savoring all that the world has to offer, while creating a beautiful home wherever he is.

Our youngest son Rodrigo, wrote about his dual identity, the difference between how he looks, his physical appearance, and who he is, his cultural identity and background. Being born in Mexico, while having white skin, blond hair and green eyes, has created that dichotomy and identity evolution as he experienced the biases and perceptions from those around him as he lived in both places. Here is the full essay:

Rodrigo León-Ramos
College Essay

Toothpaste and orange juice.
Religion and government.
Diets and Thanksgiving dinner.

Though varied, this set of combinations has a unifying theme: each pair epitomizes #TwoThingsThatDontMix. When this dichotomous hashtag took over the Twittersphere last Spring, I felt compelled to partake in the trend with a duo of my own...

@Rodrigolr12: #TwoThingsThatDontMix How I look and who I am.

Polarity has played a defining role in my identity for as long as I can remember. From the moment the doctor handed my mother her blonde-haired, green-eyed baby, my appearance has baffled virtually anyone I encounter.

Indeed, I am a white Mexican and I've been made aware of this fact for as long as I've known how to differentiate colors. I remember walking through Mexico City as a kid with my raven-haired, almond-eyed family, feeling the gazes of strangers land on me: "Güero!", they'd call out, asking if I was adopted (as if recessive genes don't exist) and making me question why I looked like an outsider next to my own family.

When we moved to the U.S., my identity crisis was flipped inside out. Suddenly, I was sitting in a classroom in Ohio—3,000 miles from home—where most of the other kids looked just like me. Besides my name, there was no obvious marker as to who I was and where I came from. For the first time in my life, no one was questioning my façade; but at that moment, I wanted to look like my family more than ever. I didn't want to blend in because, although I physically resembled my classmates, much of what they couldn't see defines who I am.

I wanted to make it known that I am a first-generation immigrant, that Spanish is my first language, and that the fabric of my identity is made up of the bold colors and sounds of my country—so that's exactly what I did. I shared my culture every chance I got, wearing my Mexican jersey more times than my mother could wash it.

After years of living in Ohio, my selfhood expanded beyond just a chilango who bleeds green, white and red; eventually, I welcomed blue into my bloodstream. Fall afternoons were filled with bonfires and hayrides, summers with Independence Day barbecues, and weekends with basketball matches and epic rap battles. I learned that the conflicting sides of my identity could not only coexist, but that they could serve as a cross-cultural bridge. I now lead the chants at football games with the same pride and gusto as when I belt the Mexican National Anthem. At family parties, my friends supply their best salsa dancing attempts followed by a confident Cupid Shuffle. Some weekends, I scarf down my mother's entomatadas, others, I devour funnel cakes at the church fair. Who I am and what I look like—two facets that caused so much inner turmoil as a 9-year-old juggling cultures—now form a perfect partnership.

That isn't to say that this has always been easy. In 2016 a swell of racism crashed down on minorities. Acts of hatred were given a platform to stand firmly upon. None of these acts were directed towards me.

"Dude, you're so lucky you look American."

The disconnect between my appearance and heritage could provide the camouflage to avoid difficult conversations. I could stand idly by as the rest of my community suffered but, just as when I first moved to the U.S., I refused to blend in. I believe it is especially important to be fearless and celebrate diversity when it seems most difficult. In times like these, it is paramount that we search for the links between things that may not mix at first glance. So, I blend the dichotomy of my identity as a platform of my own: to accept, to include, to educate, to lead, and ultimately, to find the ways in which our differences #mix.

Now, a few years after finishing college, I see how he has seamlessly blended both cultural backgrounds into his everyday life and how he genuinely enjoys his bicultural heritage. Out of our three kids, I can say he is the one who expresses most vividly his Mexican heritage and his US heritage through his customs and interactions with friends and family.

Like many things in life, we can find hidden treasures in places that are not easily recognizable as such. College essays are one of those unique jewels for a family to discover. They are a wonderful reflection of family roots and wings. My wish is that this beautiful part of the college admissions process remains, and when families are presented with the opportunity to engage, they choose to enjoy the process, to learn more about their family members and cherish the essays as beautiful memories of their upbringings together. And I extend this invitation to anyone who has ever written a college essay or helped a family member to write one, to rescue it, resurface it, read it again and talk about that young human being, who was reasserting their own personality and preparing to take on the world!

Key Takeaways:

College essays are a "rite of passage" for teenagers to reflect on who they are and who they want to be as adults.

These are wonderful opportunities to connect with them to relive their history and discover their essence, to learn more about their dreams, goals and values, and how their family roots are present in their lives.

Give the entire college application process the utmost importance and especially the college essays. Get involved, be curious and supportive. Do not abdicate or see it as a "requirement" only.

Songs:

"This is Me" – Keala Settle

"Don't Stop Me Now" – Queen

"Best Day of My Life" – American Authors

FOMO, YOLO, JOMO – Focus on What Really Matters

"If you want to live a happy life, tie it to a goal, not to people or things." – Albert Einstein

Let's face it, we all do the endless browsing on Instagram to see what is happening in someone else's life and the quest to give and get "likes" or trying to get the perfect caption for our posts, finding the trendy #hashtag, and choosing appropriate comments for the posts of those around us. On top of that, we are constantly watching the overflowing content of all kinds of cute babies, cute animals, dance trends, challenges, people making tricks, scaring each other, tripping or falling down, and so many things that suck our attention to that tiny screen, on many occasions, for hours at a time.

I do not deny the benefits of having a social media platform to share what is happening in our lives. As I mentioned earlier, it can be a positive asset to share exciting news with the people we love and that is worth continuing. The tricky part comes when whatever you are watching becomes a source of anxiety or stress. We all can think of a moment when we felt FOMO (Fear of Missing Out) for scrolling down and seeing posts of the things others do and we are not doing, the long list of places that "must visit before you die" and in particular the events and activities that those closer to you (or those who used to be close) are doing while you feel kind of stuck in your regular life, going through your daily grind of responsibilities. To make matters worse, this constantly feeds a desire to post something, to show others what a wonderful life you have, and in a very subconscious way, make them feel FOMO as well. Yes, we all do this too.

When the FOMO feeling kicks in, you wonder if you are where

you want to be, if you need to just drop everything and go. That's when YOLO (You Only Leave Once) takes over and throws you into an anxiety loop where you feel the rush to make things happen, all of them, as fast as you can. It reminds me of my son's Fernando's favorite movie, **Ferris Bueller's Day Off**, which depicts a sassy highschooler who has an uncanny skill at cutting classes and getting away with it. Ferris pretty much decides to live on a constant state of YOLO, he has two best friends, a girl named Sloane that matches his crazy energy, and a boy named Cameron, who suffers from anxiety and is very much afraid of an over controlling father, and is always trying to live up to his parents and societal expectations. Through the "day off" Ferris pushes Cameron to stop having FOMO and live a day in a pure state of YOLO. At the end of the movie, Cameron frees himself mentally from his shackles and gets a newly found courage to face his father and start living on his own terms. Then Ferris coins a phrase that pretty much summarizes what FOMO and YOLO stand for: "Life moves pretty fast. If you don't stop and look around once in a while, you could miss it." – Ferris Bueller.

Like Cameron's journey, we can credit FOMO and YOLO, or the "Ferris Bueller effect" for the "great resignation" of talent that fled from their jobs pretty much globally as the COVID-19 pandemic subsided. In particular the young talent. That was a turning point for realizing how important it is for everyone to live meaningful, balanced lives, every day, and the need to stay connected socially, virtually or in person. It normalized the need to pay attention to mental health for everyone.

As a Human Resources leader, I can tell this was a wake-up call for all business leaders and managers everywhere. It did not matter at all the type of company, the country culture, the particular profession or career field, or even the age. YOLO pretty much spread widely and changed corporate and institutional culture, policies and practices everywhere. Talent globally had for once the opportunity to live a shared human experience of rethinking their lives and revisiting how congruent their choices were with what mattered most for them and took deliberate action. So many people decided to leave their jobs, relocate to where they truly wanted to live, took leaves of absence and decided to start something new, more aligned with their purpose and interests in life, and simply decided to stay in YOLO for a while. This was painful for economies and companies but in my view, it normalized the importance of personal wellbeing as an essential element of any institutional culture, human resources programs and leadership and management expectations. Now it is not by exception, it is a base expectation that everyone must care about their employees' wellbeing and that is a great unintended consequence of the pandemic.

The risk of FOMO and YOLO combined is the addictive component. While I subscribe to living a life better connected with meaning and purpose, that has to be the ulterior motive, and not just to show off how wonderful things are. If at the end of the day, someone who is "on" FOMO and YOLO still feels stressed, anxious and empty, doing all that stuff that believed was the answer to feel more satisfied and happier, then there is a need for deeper reflection, beyond the tasks and activities themselves and redefine their approach to what it means to enjoy life and be happy.

As parents of a FOMO/YOLO generation, we are constantly learning to adapt and respond to how our kids experience these feelings as social media became more prevalent in their lives. We realized how important it is to talk about it, to listen, to understand when they felt that FOMO, and to help them stay grounded enjoying what they have, to live the present day and to be grateful and express it in their very own way.

Our daily ritual at dinner of "highs" and "lows" on how their day had been, which we continued to do well into their teenage years and presently in their adult life whenever we meet, does wonders on this. Finding ways to disconnect from social media, either by limiting the time we all spend on it and even deliberately cutting it out completely, also helped. Going out to be in contact with nature, investing our time together and enjoying the moment also helped. Constantly talking about what motivates them, learning about their goals and aspirations and being curious about how they plan to bring them to life and supporting them also helped a lot.

Having a goal related to something they really want to experience in their lives, working for it, saving the money for it, planning who they want to bring along, or just themselves, helps to eliminate the desire for instant gratification which adds to the FOMO effect. I believe that learning to wait for something you really want and working hard to get it develops your character and gives you the resilience needed to live a happy life, no matter what the circumstances might be.

Another important skill to learn and practice to deal with FOMO and YOLO is the art of saying "no" and be ok with it, without feeling any regret or guilt for making the decision to not do something just because others are doing it. This involves also learning to say no to some relationships that can be toxic and pile on to the stress of feeling FOMO by making the person actually feel excluded or rubbing onto them what they missed when they did not participate. This is why it is so important to get to know the friends and acquaintances that surround our kids, to help them identify and make decisions about who they want to keep in their lives and have the courage to decide to sever those relationships that can be harmful. This is much easier said than done, and requires courage, empathy and perseverance from the parents and the entire family.

As I'm writing this book, I recently stumbled on a new term, called JOMO (Joy of Missing Out) as a way to address the constant feeling of FOMO. The intent of JOMO is to focus on self-care, disconnecting from social media and reconnecting with being present, enjoying the moment. I am happy to see that these concepts are becoming more broadly shared, and more people realize how important it is to be intentional and mindful of the role that we choose to give social media and to focus on what really matters most in our lives.

I guess Billy Joel got it right about FOMO and YOLO on his "Vienna" song: "Slow down, you crazy child, you're so ambitious for a juvenile, but then if you're so smart, tell me why are you still so afraid? Where is the fire? What's the hurry about? you better cool it off before you burn it out.... Slow down, you are doing fine, you can't be everything you wanna be before your time... Slow down, you crazy child and take the phone off the hook and disappear for a while, it's alright, you can afford to lose a day or two..." I love this and I understand it has become pretty much an anthem for the FOMO/YOLO/JOMO generation. We can take this advice and put it into practice with ourselves and help our loved ones along the way.

Key Takeaways:

FOMO/YOLO/JOMO are symptoms of the importance of self-care and wellbeing. Finding what truly matters in our lives and being congruent with our choices about where we spend our time and who we relate to is a way to handle those expectations.

Constantly talking about this with our kids is the way to understand what is behind their feeling of FOMO/YOLO/JOMO. The label is not important, their emotion and thought process is what truly matters so we can be there and support their choices.

Songs:

"I Lived" – One Republic

"Vienna" – Billy Joel

"Solo Se Vive Una Vez" - Azucar Moreno

Finding a Prince/Princess,
and Slaying a Few Dragons Along the Way

"Love is not finding someone to live with;
it's finding someone you can't live without." – Rafael Ortiz

When our daughter Andrea was barely 2 years young, she started to fantasize about finding her "prince" to marry. I guess the Disney movies influence gets to the kids and plants that seed early on. At the time, she could not even say the word "Principe" (prince in Spanish), she would say "Cípipe", and we all laughed, at both, how it sounded, and at the idea that a 2-year-old could be thinking about marriage. Fast forward more than 25 years and no matter how she says it, it is not that funny anymore, at least not to me. Every time a new boyfriend showed up, I got a feeling in my stomach, like I needed to act, to protect her. As a father, the bar you set for anyone to be worthy of for your daughter is incredibly high. No one would be smart enough, strong enough, caring enough, considerate enough, hardworking enough, loyal enough...you get the picture. It has taken a lot of learning and growing up, from my end, to be able to accept the fact that one day, she will actually find her prince, and it will be entirely her decision, according to her own standards, and that I have an opportunity to help her in the process.

While I've been accused by my wife of having a "double standard" in many things as it comes to our daughter and our sons, we both agree that is not the case on the matters of helping them choose their life-partners. Our bar is incredibly high for all. As parents, we want our kids to live happy lives and to do so, they need wonderful human beings as partners by their side forever. This is, by far, the most important decision they will make in their lives.

What can a parent do to help their kids choose wisely? The very first thing is to decide to accompany them in their romantic relationships. It is one of the most difficult things a parent would ever do, and takes a lot of trial and error, learning and adjusting as you go along. From the moment they say for the first time "I like someone..." till the day they chose a life partner, it is a rollercoaster filled with twists and turns. You hear in your brain something like a Shakespeare phrase, a bit adapted from the "To be or not to be": "To get involved or not get involved", "To talk about stuff or to stay back and let them come to you", "To give them advice or not", "To share your opinion about their boyfriends, girlfriends, or not". These are daunting questions.

I can say that in our case, we've decided to get involved, from the beginning, from the position of unconditional love and with the role of being a coach, which we still have the privilege to do. Don't get me wrong, we realize they are in the driver's seat and calling the shots, but we can be on the co-pilot seat helping them navigate instead of just watching the car passing by from the street. This is such an important area of their lives that we realized we could not be on the sideline or just learn about what is happening after the fact. The risk of not being with them as things happen in real time is too high. Here are a few things that we learned about what we can do to help them in the process:

Talk about it, don't ignore it. From the first "puppy love" to the "forever love" we've found it is incredibly important to talk about it, but not to just talk to them about it. It is more of a "listen to them about it" and be fully engaged and emphatic on what they are feeling to help them navigate and make decisions. Asking questions that show care and do not pass judgment, like: "Is there anyone you are interested in?" "How did you get interested?" "What do you feel when you are around that person?" and match or complement their level of emotion. If they show excitement, be excited, if they feel awkward, show empathy so they feel safe to tell you more. In this area, my wife is an absolute master, always staying up to date with what is going on in their relationships. Given her skill in this area, she would be the go-to person first, and I would also engage to support and to talk more deeply when they wanted to get advice or just hear another point of view. It takes a combination of patience, persistence and tactfulness to initiate the conversation and keep them interested in sharing. It also requires parents to know when to step back and leave them space or when not to talk about something.

<u>Get to know their love interests</u>. No matter how "silly" the relationship may seem, bring them in, get to know them as soon as possible. Contrary to the belief that it may make things "too formal" by having them "meet the parents", getting to know those who are around your precious kids is the smartest thing to do. Like any of their friends, this is a way to see how they think, who they are and what kind of values and principles they display. When our kids had a date, we always insisted on bringing them home first. We set a clear rule that their dates needed to step out from their cars, come into the house, so we could meet them before going out. Our daughter can tell a few stories about how this made their boyfriends feel…. In the same light, we set the same rule for our sons to do the same when they went out to pick up their dates at their homes, to park the car, step out, go into the house and meet the parents every time. No double standard here either. By the way, this differentiated them from many other kids through the eyes of the parents of their dates, as most commonly, what happened is that kids just texted their dates to come out when they arrived at their homes to pick them up.

<u>Help them think and realize on their own what matters most instead of telling them what to do</u>. It is the parent's worst nightmare to think about your kids ending up in a bad lifelong relationship. On more than one occasion my wife and I have seen the alarm signs of a highly likely terrible outcome if our kids had chosen to stick to a bad relationship. Looking back, I can tell the biggest risk is how vulnerable they are when

they are lovestruck, you can say in many ways, they are truly blindly in love. When their closest friends and family all see the warning signs, and contrary to what we all see, they keep feeling and thinking that either things will get better supported by their love, or that they are capable of magically inducing a life change in their partner for the better, when we all know that is not going to happen.

So how do you help them "slay" these dragons disguised as "prince or princess"? It is not an easy feat. It requires getting closer to your kids and to the "dragons" in question, sharing time together doing things they both enjoy doing, so later on you can find a way to talk about it. All you can do is find ways to make them pause and think and add some perspective that takes them a bit into the future they are headed towards. To help them go deeper, to understand that as important as "love-the feeling" is, it is "love-the verb" (the actions) and putting those actions into perspective. This does not have to be confrontational, it is all about helping them go deeper, by inviting them to talk about values and potential situations in life: losing jobs, how they handle money, having kids or not, how to educate them, to learn more about their relationship with their extended families, getting to know their friends, how to deal with crisis, how to respond to an emergency, how to support them in a moment of pain or sorrow, being curious to talk about goals and ambitions for each one, their purpose in life, etc. To truly listen without being judgmental and always reinforcing that ultimately it is their decision and reminding them of the fact that they will own whatever consequences come from it.

With our kids, we created a simple metaphor for them to remember since they started going out with potential love interests, we told them "Find a motor, not an anchor for your life". And we explained why it is important to have someone who would not only support your goals but will literally help you put them in motion instead of pulling you down. Being a "motor" person is someone who will want to go places, who has passion in life, who has goals and aspirations of their own and cannot wait to share those with someone they love and create shared experiences together. An "anchor" person does not like change, is scared to go places, to take risks, to take chances in life. It is someone who depends on the other person to do most of the work and finds reasons to bring the other person's dreams down.

<u>Set an example with our behavior, with our actions as a couple</u>. If there is one thing I learned from my father, it is how he treats my mom. To this day, I keep learning from them how to have a beautiful relationship where they continue in love after being together for almost 60 years. I have never heard my father raise his voice to my mother, ever. This is something I brought to my own marriage, and it has been a cornerstone in how my wife and I have chosen to communicate. It has been amazing to witness how our kids have learned it by watching it in our lives. In their relationships they know that conflicts can be solved without fighting, without damaging each other. There has been more than one instance when our kids have shared with us that they have talked about this behavior as they have interacted with their boyfriends and girlfriends in turn. Setting an example is not only about the good stuff. It is also about how to deal with tough situations and talk about it with them. Whatever you do as a couple leaves an impression on your kids. Either consciously or subconsciously they are experiencing it, and they can choose to either emulate it or intentionally reject it if it is something they did not like.

Setting the example is also talking about things that are timeless values, and other things that change with time. What we did when we were young does not necessarily translate or make sense to our kids, but the important thing is to talk about it, to listen to what they believe, and extract their learning so they can decide what to look for in a relationship. For instance, with our kids, we talked about the meaning of Sex and Love. Our way to look at it is that in a relationship, we hope they'd consider this flow:

"Know->Feel->Do" where you first want to know the person, develop a strong relationship where you have deep feelings for each other, and then you express the love profoundly, and make love, have a sexual relationship. When all the media around shows the exact opposite flow: "Do->Feel->Know" where first two people meet randomly, have sex, they focus on that feeling of instant gratification on a more physical level and later on they worry about getting to know the person, being scared to show their real self after that level of intimacy and be reluctant to develop strong feelings of affection and long-term commitment to each other. We talked about it in these terms with our kids and shared our example as a couple who lived it that way, with the hope they consider this in their relationships.

As time has passed and we've had several rounds with our kids on this, we have seen them learning from their experiences and already making great choices to bring wonderful human beings to share their lives together. While there are still many steps along the way, we fully trust in their ability to make the right choices. We continue to focus our energy on accompanying them in the process, being involved, talking about it, getting to know their love partners, helping them think about their future to have perspective, and hoping that our example has given them clear guidance on key ingredients to consider in the process.

Key Takeaways:

The decision of who will be the life partner for our kids is the most important decision in their lives.

As a parent, getting involved in this decision, in the way that they need it (not in the way that we need it) is paramount so parents can provide the support, the wisdom and feeling of trust they need.

This is an art, not a science and involves a lot of trial and error, perseverance and adaptability from the parents.

Songs:

"Zanesville, Ohio" – Andy Leon

"Breadcrumbs" – Andy Leon

"The Stack" – Jack Rabbit

"This Again" – Jack Rabbit

*"End the Daydream (from **Fitting In** Original Movie)" – Jack Rabbit*

"Can't Help Falling in Love" – Elvis Presley

"Si tú la quieres" – David Bisbal

"Por el resto de tu vida" – Christian Nodal, TINI

"Making Love Out of Nothing at All" – Air Supply

From Ally to All-In

"The glory of creation is in its infinite diversity
and the way our differences combine
to create meaning and beauty." – Spock & Kirk

I grew up in a Catholic family in Mexico, surrounded by a social construct where everyone had very homogeneous beliefs and where there was an unveiled expectation of conformity and compliance with the same ideals, rituals and traditions. As you have read in this book, I am a proponent of rituals and traditions, as long as you believe in the essence they represent and are congruent with how you live your life. I do not subscribe to just following what others say or being pushed by the inertia of social/ peer pressure. I believe in the importance of understanding the substance and exercising the right to choose how to behave and what to support according to your personal values.

I also believe that personal values are forged as a combination of the things we learn from the example we receive from those role models we have access to, like our parents, our family members, our mentors and others who influence us with their behaviors, and also very importantly, by the experiences we live. While our core essence is pretty much set early in life, it can be molded by expanding our views of the world, by going out of our comfort zones and learning what we do not know, seeing what we have never seen, by doubting and questioning who we are and by surrounding ourselves with people who are entirely different from who we are. You learn to accept others for who they are and, in the process, learn to accept the person you are becoming as well.

Since I was around 5 years old, I had a neighbor friend whose family was from Japan. His parents immigrated from Japan, and he was a first generation Mexican, his family spoke Japanese at home and followed all the Japanese traditions. I recall going to his house as a little kid and being fascinated with the entire experience. I had to take my shoes off and leave them outside; the furniture was minimalistic, you could sit on the floor to have tea and to play; everything was neat, perfectly ordered, and the decoration of every room looked entirely different to what I was used to. This is where I tasted for the first time, real Japanese food, cooked at home and I was hooked on it for life as one of my favorite foods. Ever since, I started to think about what it would be like traveling to Japan to learn more about the culture and people. When I was in high school, my friend and I talked about getting a scholarship to go and study together in Japan for a year. I did not go through with it, but the conversations sparked a change in me, it awakened my desire to go and live abroad, to travel the world and to have experiences with other cultures.

I believe it was this desire that subconsciously attracted me to a company that offered an international career. Fast forward 34 years, I had the chance to live and work in four different countries, travel to more than 40 countries so far, and interact with people from all walks of life from all over the world. These experiences along with my chosen career field in Human Resources have definitely expanded my views of the world and my views of people and molded my personal values.

It has been truly a privilege to be able to learn so much about others and also to be trained in how to accept, embrace and value the differences from other human beings, as those differences are precisely what make a family, an enterprise, a company, and our society a better place to be, a better place to live. By honoring the individuality and unique contributions of everyone and recognizing our essence and what binds us together in the things that matter, is how people can flourish, businesses thrive, and our communities prosper.

One of the trainings that I value the most is related to Diversity,

Equality and Inclusion where a key concept is how to be a good "Ally" for people who experience the feeling of being excluded, of being a minority. A good "Ally" would do things like learning and educating themselves about the needs of others, through listening more than speaking and being open to accepting feedback on their misconceptions and biases. An ally would ask questions when they do not understand something instead of judging or assuming their own mental model and perceptions are true. Allies also reflect on their own privilege, to understand that things that they take for granted are not accessible to everyone and by doing so, engage and take action to make a difference in their own behavior to drive change.

Not only have I learned this well, but I've also taught it in leadership development programs. I had the opportunity to support, coach and engage in many situations where individuals did not feel included or valued for who they were and helped them and their managers find a way forward. I felt I had been making a difference as an informed and supportive ally.

One thing life taught me is that it is not enough to be a supportive ally to make the transformation that is needed in our society. I believe we need to step-up our game and move from being allies to be "all-in". What does it mean to be all-in? You need to make it personal, make it your cause and live it in your own life, 24/7, in every relationship and conversation you have, so it becomes a core part of your beliefs, of who you are. It is not enough to be supportive, to participate in activities, volunteer and do other things, and when you end the activity, the training, the rally, you go back to your "normal life", you take the "ally hat" off and experience a different reality.

I learned this lesson several years ago as things became much more personal and happened in my own family. The first example of this is my view of tattoos. I have to admit, I am not a fan; to be more precise, I dislike the concept. It is not a religious thing; it just does not sit well with me the idea of scarring yourself permanently regardless of whatever beautiful design or worthy personal meaning anyone can attribute. Growing up in a very homogeneous social group, the concept of having tattoos was entirely foreign to me. If anything, I was only exposed to it when watching movies as something that the "bad guys" would usually do. As I went out into the world, traveled, lived in different countries and interacted with many cultures, I became an ally on this subject, moving from having a total rejection to the idea, to having acceptance and understanding of why people do it. And when my three kids decided to get tattoos, I knew this was very personal and would become a constant in our family life interactions. As strange as it was for me in the beginning and as much as I argued with them the many reasons why I believed it was not a good idea for them, ultimately, I realized this was important for them, they chose to do it consciously, when they were adults, with a clear meaning, so I chose to accept it. I learned to respect their personal choices and made my own peace with it. As I am writing these words and reflecting on how I feel about tattoos, I think on this one I am still an ally, not all-in yet, but making good progress.

The second and more transformational example is when a few years ago my son Fernando shared with me that he is gay. From my side, I felt like there was no preamble for this conversation, one day he felt compelled to tell us, as he was already dating and wanted us to be aware and to know it from him directly instead of finding out about it through others or through posts in social media. I recall the moment he was sharing it with me and telling me about a boy he liked, how he met him, and I asked him if this was recent, if he was still in discovery of his own sexuality or if this was something he knew for some time and was clear about it. I could feel the weight and meaning of what was being shared in the tone of his voice and his words.

As he confirmed that this is who he has always been and his early discovery process in his life, somewhere in my heart and in my head an "all-in" switch turned on instantly and permanently.

I knew that this conversation was going to have a significant impact on my son's life, in our relationship as father and son, in our family life, in our extended families and with anyone close and dear to us. In that moment the only thing that I could feel was unconditional love, and that is what I expressed to him responding: "I love you my son, thank you for telling me directly. All I want for you is to have a fulfilling life where you can be who you are, flourish in every area of your life and have everything that makes you happy. I want you not to limit yourself in any way, and I also want you to always be protected from any danger that may come your way. I want you to know that you can count on me to be on your side always".

He had this same conversation with my wife and with his siblings and seeing how each of us responded with pure love and support was one of the most beautiful things we've experienced as a family. Then we started to talk about how he wanted to share this with the extended family and friends, and our "all-in" journey together began.

We've had a lot of self-discovery from everyone involved, with significant learning and reflection of how our lives had been all along. For instance, I've thought a lot about the things that I've said, or did not say before we had this news, how I could have made him feel in any given situation in the past, and the things I could have done differently to lead to an earlier disclosure and support. We've also had our fair share of reality as we see every day what is happening around us, socially and politically.

While it has not always been easy to bring others along given the nature of their own cultural upbringing expectations, the ignorance, limiting beliefs and socially embedded microaggressions that even our close friends and family members had been accustomed to carry on or participate, when you choose to be "all-in" from that moment forward the path on how to behave and what to do with them and anyone becomes amazingly clear at every turn. The choice to love and support your son for who he is becomes the only thing that matters, and it is what prevails in every situation, in every conversation, and in every circumstance around it.

One very important and beautiful gift that our son Fernando has given to our entire family by being the first to come out is to open a door for other family members to be able to do the same if that is their case. He has become a role model for others to follow. This is priceless as it has normalized it and has given the opportunity to anyone to follow in his footsteps. I am forever grateful to my son for this.

My journey moving from being a supportive ally to being "all-in" on all things that truly matter and with all the people I encounter in my path continues as a life-long endeavor. Every day I feel better prepared than the day before as I keep learning more about others and more importantly, I learn more about myself as I continue to reach out and step away from my comfort zone in all areas, seeking "progress, not perfection", so, I guess I will continue struggling a little bit longer with the idea of my loved ones getting tattoos, but eventually I will get there.

Key Takeaways:

Learn to appreciate those who are entirely different from yourself. Go out, travel, learn about other cultures and people.

Be curious, inquire, invite, reach out and ask for feedback on your own biases and blind spots.

It is not enough to be an "ally", choose to be "all-in" 24/7 and support everyone for whom they are. There is no half-way engagement. Your actions will speak louder than your words.

Let your kids teach you and show you the way. The world we grew up in has evolved; what was not openly shared in our days, it is now. Our kids know much more about it than we do, in a way pretty similar to how a kid almost intuitively knows how to interact with technology, they have grown in a world where not only is it more accepted to talk about differences, but they also expect it as they live it every day. Both my wife and I have learned a lot from our kids as we have seen how they naturally integrate and interact with everyone. When you have a question, in addition to doing your own research, ask and talk about it with your kids, listen to their advice, you will learn a lot.

Let your unconditional love be your compass at every turn.

Song:

"Malibu" – Miley Cyrus

Do What You Love, Love What You Do

*"If you love what you do, you'll never work
a day in your life"* - Confucius

The answer to the typical childhood question: "What do you want to be when you grow up?" has definitely changed a lot since it was asked to my parents when they were little kids, to when it was asked to me by my parents, to when my wife and I have asked it to our own kids.

In our parents' generation, there were more narrowly defined career fields (Doctor, Engineer, Architect, Lawyer, Artist, and a few others). In our generation, things started to get more interesting with a lot more variety of degrees and possible professional endeavors. My first memory of what I wanted to be when I grew up had to do with sports. I played soccer literally every day of my life since I was 4 years old until I was in college. My mom tells me the first answer I gave to this question is that I wanted to be a professional soccer player. In my school years, I realized that I was very good at math and science, and I also loved the human aspect of being on teams and the importance of service to others. When it was time for me to choose a profession, I actually had the chance to pursue becoming a professional soccer player but decided not to take that path. I believed the risk of focusing on sports alone without a college degree was not the best option as an injury could terminate a sports career prematurely. I chose not to attempt to do sports professionally and a college degree simultaneously so, despite being my first childhood aspiration, I chose the safer path of pursuing a college degree leaving sports as a hobby.

I narrowed the college degree options to three choices: Industrial

Engineering, Psychology, and Education. While my heart was in Psychology or Education, I chose to go for Industrial Engineering as I rationalized it was the "more employable" career, one with higher probability of professional advancement and higher levels of income which is what I had learned it was considered as higher chances of achieving professional success.

I completed my college degree in Industrial Engineering with honors and indeed, it gave me the opportunity to be hired at an international company who was looking for young talent for the start-up of a new manufacturing plant in Mexico City. Since my very first assignment at this manufacturing plant, I gravitated towards working with teams and being interested in solving the problems that other people had at work and in their lives and helping make things better for the company through helping make things better for the company by helping employees to succeed.

I realized this gave me much more satisfaction than working with any production system as an Industrial Engineer. Luckily for me, the company also realized this and found it valuable to further develop me in this area, to the point that it ended up offering me the opportunity to learn and grow in a career as human resources leader, which I did for most of my almost 34 years with the company. Within this career, I realized that the things I enjoyed most doing were: teaching others, coaching, mentoring, and working with teams, which are the very same things that I wanted to do when I considered studying Psychology or Education, so I ended up going full circle to the place I was meant to be from the start.

I tell this story for two reasons: 1) To reflect on the importance of finding what we love doing as a key part of the decision of where we want to focus our professional efforts and to go for it without hesitation, and 2) To know that it is perfectly ok to change, as many times as needed, until you find a way to do what you love for a living.

For our kids' generation, things have gotten quite more complex. Not only has the variety and number of college degrees exploded, the idea of being an entrepreneur, a social media influencer, a gig economy worker, a coder, a data scientist, a gamer, and so many other variations are in the mix of options to consider. For many of these career alternatives, you need a college degree, and for many others having a distinct talent, self-discipline and some foundational infrastructure is all you need to get you going.

We started having this conversation with our kids more seriously as they finished elementary school and entered high school. Our intent was to help them as early as possible to discover and pursue what they were more passionate about while also being good at it, so they could choose to do what they love and live a happy and fulfilling life, and we could focus on providing the support means for them to fine tune their choices.

We gave each of our children an opportunity to invest a week at the end of their sophomore high school year in a career camp at a university that offered the degree that they thought they wanted to do. Here are their stories:

From a very early age, our daughter Andrea discovered her love for music, singing and performing. After watching her perform at every possible school play, when she was a sophomore in high school, she told us she wanted to do musical theatre for life. Off she went to an Acting and Theater camp in New York. From there, she reaffirmed her conviction and dedicated the rest of her high school years to being ready to be accepted at a performing arts school in Boston. She even got a scholarship in the Honors program and went on to enjoy her college years very much. In her last semester, the school offered the option to finish her studies at their campus in Los Angeles to be much closer to the acting industry and job opportunities. She went on and decided to become an actress right after college. After working for several months at a casting agency and trying her luck at the auditions as an actress, she realized that it was not what made her happy. She decided to take a break and volunteered at a minority-owned and led, wonderful kindergarten school as a music teacher. From there she discovered her passion for education and became one of the best teachers at that school, but not having a degree in education became limiting so she decided to pursue her master's degree in education. All along this journey, she continued making music, singing and performing, which reaffirmed her passion and skills as an artist, being on stage sharing her talent with the world, while also teaching kids in her very own particular way, incorporating music, acting and helping kids develop self-confidence, social conscience, and self-growth. Today she is dedicated to developing her musical talent and portfolio, performing live with her band called "Jack Rabbit" as much as possible and releasing new music and videos constantly. In parallel, she is producing and developing her digital education show to offer to different potential clients (schools, networks, non-profits).

Our son Fernando also thought he knew at a very young age, around 11 or 12, what he wanted to be. He decided that he wanted to be an Architect and was pretty sure that is what he was born to do. Off he went to an Architecture Camp in Pennsylvania and confirmed that it was his chosen field. He worked hard for the rest of his high school years and also got a scholarship to study architecture at several schools. As he completed the first year doing very well in academic grades, he realized that it was not his passion. He talked to us asking if he could switch majors to something else. The message we shared with him was that it is always much better to know what you really want to be and change now, instead of continuing through a path that he knows is not going to make him feel fulfilled professionally and personally and many years into his professional career, decide to change because of frustrations and unhappiness. He realized that what attracted him the most to architecture was the design skills. So, he decided to switch to a Public Relations Major with a minor in Communications and Design and another one in Entrepreneurship which better lined up with his skills and strengths. His chosen areas of specialization landed him a string of jobs in the digital streaming services, working for companies such as Netflix, HBO, Roku and currently at Apple.

Our youngest son Rodrigo decided he wanted to be a Sports Management agent and a Businessman. So off he went to a Business Administration Camp in New York. He confirmed his passion for business along with his continuing desire to specialize in sports management. He worked hard for the rest of his high school years and also got several offers of scholarships and ultimately decided to go to the same school where his brother was and to the same city where his sister also was, entering the program of Business Administration. As his career unfolded, he decided not to pursue the specialization in sports management but kept his passion for sports alive with a strong desire to become an entrepreneur. As he finished his college degree he landed a job at a financial data analytics company, called FICO (Fair Isaac Corporation), where he does digital marketing. In parallel, he rediscovered another passion he had from a very young age related to design and clothing branding. This, coupled with his growing aspiration to become an entrepreneur, thrusted him to decide to start with his closest friends from high school a boutique fashion clothing business called "Kayzen Eyes (KZ)™ where amongst many things, he can devote himself to do creative designs and branding. They interact with influencers and reach out to sports athletes and music performers, while he continues to work at the technology company that offers him great flexibility and career progression.

When we look at what our three kids are doing, we feel very proud of their choices because they have been seeking to do things they love and that they are good at and have had the courage to decide to adjust their paths early on to pursue their passions in life.

With the influence and ever-expanding access of Artificial Intelligence and technology to virtually every career field, things will continue to rapidly evolve. As a parent, I can only imagine how things will change and how crucial it will continue to be to stay engaged and informed to be ready to support our children as they decide what to do with their lives. In any case, I firmly believe that we can talk more with our children about finding meaning in their lives, searching their purpose and discovering their passions; those things that make them want to wake up in the morning and do over and over again because it makes them happy, because it makes them feel alive, because they are good at them and see themselves making a difference, connecting with a higher order purpose for their lives, even if they were not paid to do it. With this in mind, we can help them be more prepared to decide what to do, to try it with their full heart in it, and if it ends up not being what they love, to find the courage to change whenever they need so they can live a happy, fulfilling and flourishing life.

It is like my mom said to me in my formative years as we talked about what I wanted to be growing up, she always responded: "I will be ok with whatever you choose to be as long as you love it, and you become the best at it. If you choose to sweep streets or collect trash for living, I want to see you doing it with excellence, with pride, smiling, singing and waving at people along the way."

I believe that job satisfaction does not depend on the task being performed, but rather on the impact it has on ourselves and on others. A clear example to describe this is the image of window washers cleaning the windows at different children's hospital buildings, where they suit up as superheroes and interact with hospitalized kids to make them smile and brighten their day. Cleaning the windows is not what matters most, it is the smile and the excitement in the kids' day what gives the most satisfaction to everyone involved. I believe that everyone can find meaning in their workday if they find a way to connect it to a higher order purpose.

Key Takeaways:

Job satisfaction does not depend only on the task performed or career field chosen, it depends on the impact it has on other people's lives.

The only expectation that truly matters from parents regarding their kids' chosen career or profession is that they find something they love doing every day. That it is aligned with their purpose in life, and that they are good at it so they can support themselves financially and live an independent life as a result of doing it.

Song:

"Good Job" – *Alicia Keys*

Bonds

"Family (noun): A circle of strength
with bonds that can't be broken.
The people you live for, laugh with and love the most."

To talk about bonds, is to remind ourselves that families are for life. Families are not a merely temporary social construct with the purpose of getting kids ready to leave and then keeping random contacts with them. Family is the most essential relationship that we all can enjoy from the moment we are born until we leave this planet for good.

For the adult kids, this means continued and accelerated growth into their full autonomy and independence, with a wonderful opportunity to continue their interdependence and support from the people who love them the most. The family bond that ties them together can be stretched as far as they need it. While they have gone out, they are not totally gone or severed from where they belong.

When I think about this stage for the parents, it means rediscovering a beautiful opportunity to continue living with a full-glass mindset (vs. empty nest): to cherish and honor the stages of roots and wings, and to enter with love and confidence into the stage of family bonds for life.

Having a family of all adults comes with new challenges like complex schedules, job demands, friends to care for, living in different locations, and many other forces that can pull the family in separate directions. It is all about continuing to be intentional about being present in each other's lives, knowing that at this stage, the initiative to get together can be a two-way street. If you miss someone, call them, if you want to see someone, visit them, if you need help, ask for it. If you want to say something, say it. Forget all the self-imposed limits and doubts. Just do it.

In this final section of the book, I share a few stories about our beliefs, rituals and actions that we intentionally do to keep those precious family bonds alive for everyone: from going away, to the traditions we continue and the decisions we have made as a family to be able to stay close to each other and stay in touch regularly.

As a family we are at this stage of life, and it is a fascinating daily learning experience. We don't get it right all the time, but we certainly do our best to make good choices with love and care for each other. Like the saying goes: "We may not have it all together, but together we have it all."

Song:

"Better Together" – Jack Johnson

Going Away, Not Moving Out

"I'll love you forever, I'll like you for always,
as long as I'm living, my baby you'll be." – Robert Munsch

I find quite interesting the way different cultures approach the moment kids reaching the appropriate age to be considered adults. In the USA, turning 18 years old legally allows you to be considered an adult. You can live by yourself, vote, get married, own a gun, but you cannot drink alcohol or rent a car. If you live in Mexico, you can do pretty much all of the above, whether you are ready for it or not.

Beyond what the law says, cultural and societal expectations bring other elements for consideration. For instance, in Mexico it is an unwritten general expectation for families to continue having their adult kids staying at home through the college years and beyond, and for the most part, leave home when they get married (if they choose to do so). The transition to adulthood is slower, given the shelter and comfort that in many ways kids and parents are perfectly fine to extend as much as possible. From the continued daily presence and support of the family to the availability of food, utilities and more importantly the stability of routines and relationships, kids continue to enjoy "being in the nest" a while longer. This comes with the price for kids to continue to abide by the family limits and rules, knowing they need to tailor their young adult freedom to these family customs. This has to do with curfews, what they can do, activities they join and, of course, the expectation to continue to attend all family events and social functions.

In the US the unwritten expectation is that kids move out when they go to college (or when they reach that age if they choose not to go to college). With that in mind, teenagers start taking jobs during summers and afternoons of their high school years to prepare as much as possible, not only by having a job to make money, but to learn work ethics and all that entails having a responsibility to show up, to learn new skills and interact with others. Also, colleges are designed to host students with rooming and boarding options for kids to stay there and in many cases, a compulsory expectation from the colleges for kids to live on campus at least the first year. In a way, it is supposed to be a time of experimenting and learning to be more independent, away from their parents, in a "controlled" environment. The idea is to have more freedom, within certain predetermined boundaries and clear accountability for their academic and professional development.

The parental approach has different views in this regard. In the US, it seems to me that for the most part, many parents believe that their job is pretty much done by the time kids go to college. Kids move out and, in many cases, parents choose to remodel the home using the now empty room or down-size to a smaller home. Other parents do keep the room intact for some time, but not necessarily with the expectation for the kids to return or live there any amount of time. It is more as a memory and to host them while they visit for the holidays. Some parents provide some financial support for college tuition, albeit it is not always the case and more often than not, you hear that kids are on their own to pay for their college tuition and all living expenses. They are considered fully grown adults the moment they leave home to go to college, and they need to take care of themselves in all senses.

Our three kids already having completed this stage, I can say we've created our own approach that incorporated the best of both worlds:

From our Mexican heritage, we chose to preserve the value of our kids feeling they have not moved out during college. They knew their home was still at the same place, and in a way, it was like they had gone to study abroad temporarily. Their room, their clothes and their overall sense of home was still in the same place. For spring break, vacations and time off, they always knew they could return home, not just as a visit, but to really go back home. We wanted them to feel that home is a place where they come back to reconnect with who they are, where they can recharge, get centered, rest and regain the strength they needed to go out again.

From the USA heritage, we chose to preserve the value of being ready to assume adult responsibilities earlier. We helped them prepare by having jobs as early as possible, during their teenage years, to make some money, to learn how to use it, to have their bank account, pay for some of their own things like their dates out with friends and love interests, and to understand the cost and value of things. No matter how much we thought we had prepared them for this, we still had some trepidation when the time came for them to go out for an extended amount of time at that young age according to our own views and upbringing. It was not easy, but we made it work.

All our kids went to college out of state. We live in Ohio, and they went to Boston and Los Angeles to study. During their college years, they always came back home. We did not have a single conversation of "moving out". To this day, whenever they come, they are and feel at home, never feeling like a visitor. On the other hand, they live in another place and have grown to be responsible for carrying their own weight and taking care of their expenses.

Our intent was to create a gradual transition, seeking a good balance between giving them as much freedom as possible with as much responsibility and accountability as needed. And more importantly, giving them a very strong bond with their home, to their roots, with a sense of belonging within the family that expanded beyond the traditional boundaries of either culture.

Key Takeaways:

As kids grow up and go out to college, having family support becomes even more important. This is a period of testing, learning and experimenting, where being able to talk things over and come home periodically is of great value for their lives.

Having freedom and autonomy is not in conflict with continuing to enjoy the warmth and care of those who love them the most.

Songs:

"My Wish" – Rascal Flatts
"Never Grow Up" – Taylor Swift

Oh! the Places We Go

"You're off to great places!
Today is your day!
Your mountain is waiting, so...
Get on your way!" – Dr. Seuss

Of all the things we choose to do as a family, I believe traveling together is at the top of the list of the most fulfilling. I guess the traveling bug caught our family very early on. In part, it was thrust upon us from all the traveling we needed to do associated with the relocation to different countries due to my job.

Our son Rodrigo holds the record of having his passport at the youngest age, when he was one week old to be precise. I remember when we went to the passport office, we could not get his photo taken right as it was nearly impossible to catch his eyes open or avoid showing my hand holding his head. We needed to do this as we relocated from Mexico City to Phoenix, Arizona when he was around 45 days old. By the time he was two years old, he probably had more SkyMiles than I did in my first 25 years of life. I have this memory of Rodrigo, probably less than 2 yrs old, crossing the airport's security metal detector and without anyone saying anything, he would stand straight, extend both of his arms, open his legs and look up at the TSA agent, waiting to be scanned with the metal detector wand. It was adorable!

The fact is that our three kids became expert travelers early. We made a point on each trip to develop their skills to be world travelers. They always carried their own mini luggage (backpacks, carry-ons), we would give them their passport at the airline counter and have them give it to the airline agent, and stay there to see how things were done, listen to the questions asked and eventually, learn how to fill in the appropriate travel forms required. They put their luggage on the scale, and once we had the boarding pass, we would teach them how to find the flight number and ask them to find the gate on the airport monitors. They learned how to go through the security checks at the airport by themselves and be on the lookout for their bags and even check for their siblings' bags. Once they found the gate on the monitors, we asked them to guide us to get there. They would take turns leading the family so we could get to where we needed to be. We did the same at train stations, bus rides, amusement parks or any other places where we needed to find our way to get there.

Since they were pre-teenagers, whenever we had a family trip, we asked them to research the destination and come up with ideas of what each suggested for the family to do, asking to include not only fun things but also cultural activities like museums, galleries and historical places. On some trips, we even asked them to plan for a day, considering the activities, finding the cost and even thinking about some of the logistics. At the location, one of them would be the "family tour guide" on how to get to the place and go through the activity.

Now as adults, we keep the family tradition of traveling together. This is actually something that we learned from my wife's family. She is one of six siblings, and her parents have the tradition of making one big trip every couple of years where all the siblings would go and have done it for as long as I have known them (more than 30 years by now), including significant others along the way. This has become something everyone looks forward to doing and the highlight of the year for my wife's parents. With all the hectic lives we all have and the multiple demands of our time, the fact that every one of their adult kids make a priority to get together and have a shared experience is very special and continues to nurture the strength of the family bond by being present in each other's lives. My wife and I decided to extend this tradition to our own family. Every couple of years we go on a big trip with our adult kids, all together. Given the complexity of our life schedules, we plan it way in advance. And the fun and bonding opportunity starts from the very first conversation about the next family trip. It brings us together to talk about schedules, possible destinations, difficulties they have to free themselves from their jobs, and to balance with other important events happening in their lives. As we plan for the trip, we get to learn and dialogue about all of those things as well.

It was very interesting for me to learn that this is actually what Disney invites families to do to have a wonderful experience at their theme parks. A few years ago, I had the opportunity to visit Silicon Valley and learn from an Argentinian company called Globant that helped Disney develop their initial concept of the "Magic wristband". Aside from the brilliance of the technology at the time, the algorithms and all the coding and data they used, we focused our learning on how they designed the ideal end-to-end user experience journey, from the very first desirable moment of interaction with the Disney brand to the last possible moment of departure and post trip contact.

The idea is that they want families to get excited about the trip and about the entire experience from the very first moment they think about going to Disney. With this in mind, they created a way for all family members to virtually interact with how to plan the trip, decide where to stay, what to eat, what parks to visit, what attractions to go, in what order, to choose if they want to have a Disney character's reserved private moment, to share if they are celebrating a special family event, and so many other things they can customize to their particular needs and wants. But the most important thing is not the variety of things they offer, but rather how much the family gets to visualize being together doing those things, the excitement it gives them to imagine how it would be, and the non-stop talking about it, dreaming about it for days, weeks and even months. By the time they arrive at the parks, there is already a significant amount of family bonding and joy experienced together.

While there are so many wonderful and amazing places to visit around the world, I believe that ultimately the destination is not what really matters. What matters most is to be intentional as a family, to be together on a regular basis, to stay connected, to choose to be present in each other's lives, to strengthen our bonds and our love. And when you are on the trip, to fully relax and enjoy the experience, to laugh, to dance, to explore and learn new things about where you are going, about the people you meet and about each other.

As I say to our family when we begin planning for our next trip, "it is time to make new memories", and of course, from the very first moment I think about the trip, I also imagine myself on the last day of the trip, when I will ask them for their help to find and bring to me their best candidate for the family heart-shaped rock as our priceless memory of another wonderful journey together!

Key Takeaways:

Traveling as a family at any age is one of the best ways to create and strengthen everlasting family bonds. The destination is not truly what matters most, it is making a priority to be with the family and having a shared experience together.

The wonderful thing about planning a family trip is that every family member starts enjoying the experience from the very first moment they talk about having the trip together and it lasts for a lifetime!

Songs:

"Oh, the Places You'll Go" – Anthem Lights
"Life is a Highway" – Rascal Flats
"Perderme Contigo" - Bacilos

Our New Roots, in a New Place, Together

*"No matter who you are or what you look like,
how you started off, or how and who you love,
America is a place where you can write
your own destiny."* – Barack Obama

When my wife and I were presented with the opportunity to work and live in another country, we did not know how much our life was going to change. At the beginning, we thought it was going to be a unique opportunity to have a broadening experience for two to three years and then return to our home country for good. We had been married for 6 years, had three little kids ages 4 years, 2 years and a newborn, and our baggage was full of love and best wishes from our extended family and friends. We also packed our wonderful home country culture, and a heritage that we were not ready to let go of (and we have never done so).

As the first assignment abroad was nearing its completion, I felt a compelling desire to go to the city where my company was headquartered globally. After being almost 13 years with the company, it felt right for me to have an experience where everything started for this company almost 190 years ago and be at the place where the purpose, values and principles of the company that I love were forged, as that is what attracted me to join and helped me stay at this wonderful place to work for more than three decades. On the family side, I felt that another two to three years abroad would not make a huge difference in the long run. The thing that happens when you make changes to your original plan is that an alternative universe is created. Unknowingly, we had just decided to materially change forever the future that my wife and I had envisioned when we got married.

Little did we know that this decision was the beginning of a very intense and fulfilling nomadic family lifestyle, changing assignments every two to three years, and moving internationally multiple times. In total, we ended up living in four countries (Mexico, USA, Brazil, Panama), 6 cities, moved homes 14 times, and lived in countless temporary places and hotels in between assignments and in between homes. Like I've shared in earlier chapters, this became our family life by choice and what our kids grew up knowing. As they became teenagers, they were consulted on important decisions about job opportunities, timings for our moves, schools to attend, new homes to move into, and all that entailed every new change for our family. They always had a voice and as they grew older, they also had a vote. As a family we decided to return to Mexico when our oldest daughter was in 7th grade, and our sons were in 5th and 3rd grade. It was a marvelous opportunity for them to reconnect with their roots, with the culture of their birthplace, with their extended family, to make new friends and to reaffirm their identity. We knew our time in Mexico was limited so we made the best of it. When our time was up to change assignments, as hard as it was for all, we decided to leave Mexico again, as we had clarity that all our kids desired to go to college in the US where they were familiar with the school system and where they saw themselves living post college. This has been one of the hardest decisions we've made as a family. It is one thing to leave your home country once, and another much more difficult is to leave your home country, return for several years and then leave again. It was as heartbreaking for us as it was for the entire extended family and friends.

As we were making this decision, life threw another wrench as I was given the opportunity to have a new job based in Singapore. At the time, it would have meant for our daughter to do her senior year of high school in another continent and then move to college in the US very far from the family. This and other factors did not fit well with the stage and aspirations of the rest of the family members so together we decided it was better to stay in the US, at the risk of my company not having another job for me there. Luckily, I was assigned to do one of those corporate jobs, one that I had not set my eyes on previously, which in the end turned out to be a great experience as well.

About the time we were returning to the US, our daughter was about to enter her senior year in high school and our kids were entering 10th grade and 8th grade. So, another big life decision was ahead of us. Our work visas and permanent residence cards were close to expiring so we needed to decide our family path for the future.

We talked about how each of us saw their lives, what we wanted to pursue, where we wanted to live and where we would like to establish our new family roots with the mindset to be located near so we can continue being present in each other's lives as much as we wanted without having to take a plane; so, we decided on living within a 2-hour radius from each other. We settled on going to the west coast in the future as it also has the added value of being more diverse culturally and closer to Mexico for our extended family visit purposes.

With this decision in mind, we pursued the process of becoming US citizens. Later on, as our kids finished their high school studies, they applied to schools all over the country, and for some magical law of manifestation and attraction, they all ended up studying in California either for their undergraduate or their graduate/master studies. With this move, our long-term family plan to establish our new family roots was set in motion.

As Rodrigo, our last son, went to college, a new adventure awaited my wife and me, with another great opportunity to move internationally, to have my dream job at the company I had worked for 27 years at the time. I was offered the chance to return to Latin America, to live and work from Panama and become the head of human resources for the entire region. And this is how our "full nesting" stage started, which I will elaborate in greater detail in the following chapter.

While the decision to move farther away, to another country for more than 5 years, seemed counterintuitive to our already decided plan to establish our family roots closer to each other, it was a well thought out detour on our part. On one hand, it provided a "new beginning" for my wife and me, a fresh start away from the place where we had seen our kids leave for college. It gave us the opportunity to expand our set of life experiences, and it was a wonderful way to bring my career to a close, reaching the desired destination I had set my eyes on for more than 25 years and finishing on a very high note.

The great thing about having clarity on your vision is that you make decisions with the end in mind. All our years abroad in Panama, we knew we wanted to return to the place where we had aligned for our family future, and we took deliberate steps towards it.

For instance, as our kids finished college, each of them went on to live with friends in shared homes, not so well maintained spaces and paying high-cost rents for small rooms, so we made a family plan to bring our three kids to live together, buying an old home that we could renovate to lower the cost of their rents and more importantly, to have a place for our entire family to live and strengthen our family bonds. This place became our first home in California, where we spent countless hours together fixing it, cleaning it and turning it into a home for the family. It is a place where we all sheltered together for weeks as we saw the COVID-19 pandemic explode. It is a place where we celebrated college graduations, birthdays, where our kids have had epic gatherings with their friends, it is a place where we have extended our family roots into a new city and are creating bonds for life there.

As my wife and I spent many trips there, we realized that as wonderful as this old-renovated home has been for our kids, it is not a long-term place for our family. We know it has been a "transition home" for them to live the stage between college and the time when they decide to start their own families.

With this in mind, during our years in Panama, my wife and I were intentional about finding a place for us as well. We did a few trips to California and Arizona to search for possible future home alternatives for us upon retirement. Being clear on our family decision of being no more than 2 hours away, we discarded Arizona and zoomed into places near Los Angeles to find our next family home, to meet our criteria of being "close enough that we can drive to see each other any day of the week, and not so far that it is not necessary to pack and ask for a vacation day at work every time our kids want to go there". With this in mind, we found our new home in Santa Clarita, just north of Los Angeles.

And this is where we are now. After having a nomadic lifestyle for the past 32 years, moving and changing places every two to three years, it is an amazing feeling to have a place where we want our roots to go deeper into our local community, where we want our family to have a new beginning and continue sharing our love and strengthening our bonds for generations to come.

Key Takeaways:

Like John Lennon said: "Life is what happens to you while you're busy making other plans" so the important thing is to have a vision for your family to stay connected and adjust the plans along the way.

Grow roots wherever you are, knowing that roots can be transferred from one place to another, and new seeds can be planted anywhere, and they will grow with care and love from each family member.

Song:

"We've Only Just Begun" – The Carpenters

"Full Nesting", Filled with Love

*"Happiness not in another place but this place,
not in another hour but this hour."* – Walt Whitman

Time does fly when you are having fun and time certainly goes at light speed when your kids are growing up. While it might not feel that way when they are very little, and you are swamped with their activities, their needs, their demands on top of the demands of your job, friends, extended family and all that entails raising a family in those early years, let me tell you that inevitably, we all realize how fast it has gone...when they are gone.

As this happens, another important realization takes place: there is life after all your kids go to college and graduate. Some people refer to this stage as the "empty nesting" part of life, when parents end up in a large home, with empty rooms where the kids used to live. This transition and the name of "empty nesting" can truly be very sad for many parents. The sense of loss is tangible and very real, you see it when you walk through the house every morning and the rooms are indeed empty, and the noisy little humans who used to live with you are not there anymore and silence prevails. For every loss, there are also gains, you have more time, you have more space, you have more experience and knowledge, and most likely, you also have more resources available.

As I mentioned earlier in the book, as we go through changes in life, human beings navigate through three phases: 1) Ending of the previous stage, 2) Transition phase, 3) New Beginning. How we choose to respond in every stage determines how long it will take to move to the next one and ultimately, moving on to the next phase in life. Some people might get stuck for a long time on the ending, mourning and missing, and slowly accepting to transition, while others might just do a "Tarzan swing" jumping directly to the new beginning, ignoring the much-needed closure and transition phases. You can see this reflected in the actions they take. Some people enter their "empty nesting" stage by deciding to downsize and move to a smaller home, others decide to remodel their home to better suit their needs. Others decide to stay where they are and not make any changes to their homes. The physical changes to the home environment are just a reflection of what people are going through in their minds and hearts. I cannot judge either approach, as it does depend on the context for each family. All I can do is to share how we have chosen to respond in our own lives.

Our core belief is that we do not have an empty nest. On the contrary, we have a full nest, full of experiences shared as a family, and full of opportunities to continue doing so. It all started with our belief in enjoying the present, to be happy wherever we are at the moment, with whomever we are now. It was followed by our conviction that the very first change we have gone through was the opportunity to reinvigorate our life as a couple, being in more control of our schedules and resources, where we can dedicate ourselves to investing more in strengthening our relationship. We planned to continue filling our nest with meaningful experiences that my wife and I want to have together, such as learning something, starting a new business venture, using our time early in the mornings or in the evenings to do sports, seeing our friends, taking on new or old hobbies and going out more.

Then we continued filling our nest with the wonderful opportunity to be in constant communication, contact and even in-person interaction with our kids wherever they might be. We have the ability to be there when they need us and when we need them. We called this the "stability with flexibility" stage, where we chose to be in a "home base" most of the time for our life as a couple, and we have the flexibility to accommodate more on our side to our kids' ever changing and busier schedules, with the mindset of being intentional, planning together to be present in each other's lives for important events for everyone or just to invest in being together as often as possible, hanging out, enjoying the simple things of life once again, like watching sunsets, walking to the park, hiking, and doing the rituals and family traditions we all love.

On top of that, we fill our nest with bigger things like traveling more, serving and volunteering in our community more and dedicating quality time with our extended families as well.

Have we made any changes to our home, to our physical "nest"? Yes, we have, but all those changes have considered how to continue making our home an ideal place for the entire family, as we continue seeing our home as the place to be together, to reunite as frequently as possible. And we will continue to do so, making room to have new family members join, and to enjoy more experiences and family traditions for years to come.

Key Takeaways:

Parents can approach the stage when the kids become adults and go away as either "glass half empty or half full". While the loss of not having the kids at home anymore is real and a proper transition is needed, there are so many positive new opportunities this stage in life brings.

The decision to be in each other's lives is a two-way street when the kids are adults. Life is too short to be waiting or to assume anything. Take the initiative, seek, call, invite, make the effort and be present.

Songs:

"Three Little Birds" – Bob Marley & The Wailers
"Conselho" – Nanda Garcia

Getting to Know Their Friends at Every Stage

"Everyone has a friend during each stage of life.
But only lucky ones have the same friend i
n all stages of life." – Ajay K. Pandey

When your kids are growing up at home, it becomes natural to get to know their friends. With all the school events, and the after-school activities such as sports, arts and crafts, and just following the calendar of events, holidays, summer camps, and impromptu gatherings with neighbors, it can be easy to see who is around your kids if you pay attention and are close to them. You get to see their interactions in real time through all those activities, and you can have meaningful content to talk about with them as you have some context and firsthand experience of what is going on in their lives.

You can also invite their friends to your home as part of the normal activities that kids do, like after a sports match, or when they go out to an amusement park, or when they go out to do some things together like trick-or-treating on Halloween. Or just as a gathering place when they go out to a nearby park and return to hang out and play videogames. This also brings a very valuable opportunity to interact with the parents of your kids' friends which can go from low-key logistical ("I'll bring my kids at this time..." "can you pick them up at this place?", etc.) to socializing together including the kids. This can evolve to very meaningful friendships between families that can last for a lifetime. You get to see and learn from different families, their values and beliefs and how those have molded the closest friends of your kids.

As your kids go off to college, it is natural and kind of expected to lose that level of proximity to their inner circle of friends.

While it is understandable that when we all grow up, we don't want to have our parents around when we are with our friends, be it in college or in our adult lives, I do believe it is important for both the grown kids and the parents to know who their closest friends are and who is around them at every stage.

This is paramount as they go out into the world on their own and begin exploring and experimenting in all areas of their lives. Finding a way to learn about what interests them and with whom they share their time and activities is something that I do not think should be seen as intrusive, or overprotective, but rather as an immense opportunity to continue sharing our life experiences with other people and a true source of enjoyment for your relationship with them.

As our kids grew up and till this day, we've always made a point in wanting to know about their friends and are open about our desire to interact with them. When we visited them when they were in college, we always asked them to bring their friends along for lunch or dinner, invite them to our family celebrations, to go out and hike, or to any plan we had for the day. When we went to see their activities at the college for special events, we also made a point of investing time in talking to their friends and their parents if they were present, in a very similar way to when they were little. Showing interest in them, asking questions about what they do, what they want in life, getting to know them for who they are and finding out what values and activities they like to share with your kids. Listening without judgement, just learning about them.

This attitude of wanting to engage and being genuinely interested in their group of friends has created a strong bond in our relationships. We have seen who their true friends are, we know them in person, and they know us. They know we care about them, and that we appreciate them for being in our kids' lives. We know we can reach out to them directly if we ever need their support to help our kids. Conversely, we've also known who those friends have been who were not the best influence in our kids' lives and by having firsthand experience and interactions with them, we could have enough context to have a meaningful conversation with our kids about who they want to keep close and what they are getting out of those relationships. This is one of the most important lessons that anyone can learn in life as in many ways who we are and what we do in life is heavily impacted by those closest to us. Making conscious choices on who to keep in your inner circle and who to stop investing in takes a lot of courage. We have seen how our kids have made decisions to "prune" or trim their group of friends and also to seek out new, positive relationships and we have been there to support them in the process as much as needed.

We've also had the privilege to see who their friends for life are, those "brothers and sisters" from other parents who have been with them through thick and thin, who have been a constant presence in their lives, through all our family moves and despite the distance, changes and all that has happened in their lives, continue to have a privileged place in their hearts and by doing so, have a very special place in our hearts as well.

Friends are such an important part of our lives that I believe it should be no mystery for families to know who they are and to have the opportunity to make them part of our ongoing family life.

Key Takeaway:

Getting to know your kids' friends at any stage in life is a great opportunity to strengthen the family bond by learning about who is important in their lives and opening up to have meaningful experiences with them.

Song:

"I'll Be There for You" – The Rembrandts

Filling the Gaps

"Don't 'mind the gap' but 'fill the gap'.
It takes a village to raise a child." - Dr. Bethany Cook

Recently I heard an oversimplification of what the essence of the role of a husband in a relationship is, boiled down to "3 P's": Provide, Protect, and Promote. I can definitely relate to these but believe they are not exclusive to the traditional role of a husband in a relationship. In our modern world, I see these as shared responsibilities of the couple as a clear way to manifest their unconditional love for each other through specific actions.

Then I kept thinking about what these would be if we add the role as parents and I would make it a total of the "7 P's": Preach with example, Prioritize, Provide, Protect, Prepare, Promote and Preserve. I know I am making a simple thing a bit more complex but that is what happens when you move from being in a couple's relationship to becoming a parent. While I think all these are pretty much self-explanatory, allow me to share a few additional thoughts.

I'll start by sharing our own family approach that I call "filling the gaps" which I believe is a never-ending responsibility of a parent. I firmly believe that it only ends when you leave this earth. As kids transition from being totally dependent on their parents to becoming mostly independent and self-sufficient, inevitably life will challenge them with situations where having the support of a parent can be invaluable. To be clear, this does not mean to continue making them dependent; on the contrary, it teaches them a lesson on interdependence, where asking and accepting help is a healthy behavior. In the same way, it opens a two-way street for the kids to also fill the gaps of their parents when they need it. This is what being a family is all about.

The gaps will come in different shapes and sizes. Sometimes there can be material gaps in things like money, financial advice, things to borrow, places to stay for a while, items they need for a special event, etc. At other times they can be emotional gaps like relationships advice, lending an ear to listen to their troubles and a shoulder to cry on, a cheerleader joining them in celebration of special moments in their lives; or a professional gap where they can use a life coach to bounce ideas on how to approach a career move, or find a way to handle a difficult boss. And of course, some of the most important gaps to fill are about family life: sharing life experiences as a parent and as part of that, sharing beautiful stories about what you did as a parent with them and the lessons learned.

With this in mind, you can see the relevance of the 7 P's. If an adult kid faces a gap in material things, Preaching with the example and helping them make choices on Prioritizing expenses can help to fill it even more than Providing the solution by lending the money (which is a valid option when needed). If the gap is emotional, Protecting them and Preparing them to regain their strength to decide what to do could be what is needed the most. If a professional gap comes along, then Prioritizing what is important in life, Promoting their values and self-worth/self-confidence could be of great help. And if they encounter a family life gap situation, then pretty much all the P's can come into play, with special attention to Preserving the relationship, focused on love and family union in whatever solution they choose to act on.

You get the point. This is not a recipe; it is more like a compass in my mind. Ultimately, those 7'Ps are engraved in your heart and will come out at the right time, you just need to listen to your intuition and think of their wellbeing at all times.

This concept of filling-the gaps with adult kids was put to the test with the most recent COVID-19 pandemic. The impact that it had on people's mental health, the way they had to adjust their jobs and working environment, or entirely changing career fields, housing availability, mobility, travel, kids going to school and much more, created major gaps in our society. I believe the first responders to solve these gaps have been the parents in every family, challenging social conventions like "adult kids shall not return to live with their parents", or people entirely redefining their career to find better balance, to live a life more aligned with their purpose, and families learning new behaviors to cope with new realities.

Some of these new coping behaviors extended beyond the pandemic and sometimes have created stress in family relationships. The concept of having adult kids still depending on their parents for help seems to continue to bother our society at some level as it may seem like a parenthood failure if adult kids return home for a while or need support to get back on their feet in certain areas of their lives.

I do not subscribe to this at all, I do believe that those gaps are just the reality of life for our kids and family continues to be there for them to help whenever they can. It's like the Japanese art of "Kintsugi" ("join with gold") which consists of repairing broken pottery by mending the areas of breakage with dusted powder mixed with gold, silver or platinum. The meaning is that breakage and repair are inherent parts of the history of an object, rather than something to disguise, hide or even reject. By adding precious metals, it highlights what has been mended and it makes the object more beautiful once restored. I think this applies to the idea of filling gaps with adult kids, where the family support is precisely the gold, silver or platinum needed to help them fill those gaps with love, and once it is filled, it makes them stronger, more beautiful and by doing so, strengthens the bond in their relationship with their family forever.

In our family we continue practicing the filling-the-gaps in all aspects of our lives, with the intent of continuing having an interdependent relationship where our three kids are now adults and carry their own weight as much as we do. We all recognize that from time to time, help might be needed and much appreciated. Be it to provide a little more knowledge on something, to lend a hand with resources or literally just being there for each other to continue having regular conversations about what is going on in our lives.

The beautiful thing that comes out of this approach is that the family gravitates to fill each other's gaps as well. It is not just from the parents to the kids; it also expands to filling gaps between siblings and having the kids filling the gaps of their parents as needed. Unplanned and unexpected reciprocity coming out of love is a natural consequence of a family that cares for each other.

Key Takeaways:

The end game of raising a family is not only for your adult kids to achieve financial self-sufficiency. It certainly is not just to get the kids out of the house and out of the family payroll. The end game is to see them living their purpose, being happy, finding the drive to pursue their dreams and enjoying fulfilling and flourishing relationships with everyone around them.

Filling the gaps with care, accountability and unconditional support is a way to stretch the family bond and love when it is needed the most.

Songs:

"Keep Your Head Up" – Andy Grammer

"Bad Day" – Daniel Powter

FAM JAM

"Communication is the lifeline
of any relationship." – Elizabeth Bourgeret

Out of all the things that I am grateful for living in this day and age, having the possibility to instantly communicate as a family using technology is high on my list. Being the last generation who grew up without this technology until we were married and had kids, this has been life changing for our nomadic family life. I still recall needing to write love letters by hand, sending them by mail, and using a rotary disk stationary telephone for a weekly call to my now wife as the standard means of communication when we were dating. Now being able to make a video call on my iPhone, right there on the palm of my hand, in real-time, to talk to my loved ones, is something that I don't take for granted.

By making this technology accessible to pretty much anyone on the planet, it has also created new challenges which I like to refer to as "mind-space/heart-space". Now it is possible to have those real-time, face-time conversations with anyone. We can create multiple chat groups to stay abreast of what is happening in the life of anyone, anytime, all the time; it is also possible to share our lives 24/7 posting every moment though a variety of social media outlets that it is hard to stay up to date with everyone that matters. When you look at anyone's phone, you easily could scroll down through multiple screens of WhatsApp chat groups with endless notifications and updates.

This is when the "mind-space" challenge shows up. How much of my mind (and time) can I dedicate to creating more and more chat groups that I can keep up with and meaningfully enjoy it? Like any "monster of our own creation" the size and scope will depend on how much we can feed it and care for it.

Then the "heart-space" challenge shows up. Which groups truly matter? Which are purely transactional (i.e. work related, kids' activities related, personal development, neighbors) that exist to give and get information, coordinate logistics, and to have low-key engagement, only when it is necessary. Out of all the chat groups that I have, which ones are most dear to me, those that truly nurture my soul and are core to further develop strong bonds in my relationships?

I think the nature of the algorithm of the apps that can host all our chats can help us answer the challenge of mind-space/ heart-space as it lists the chats in order of frequency of use. Those chats you regularly enter and engage in are the ones that constantly appear at the top of your screen. This could be a helpful first filter to analyze where I focus my attention and who I care about the most.

In our family's case, it is indisputable that the chat of our immediate family, of my wife, our three kids and myself constantly shows at the top of my screen. This chat we call our FAM JAM. It is the very first chat that I check every morning and the last one I check every night. It has become our virtual family get-together where aside from other social media platforms, we share what is going on in our lives, in a way that is consistent with our family's love languages and values and where many of our rituals show up from time to time.

This is where we get the first exclusive on the breaking news, like the launch of a beautiful new song by our daughter Andrea, or where she tells us about an inspired new film project of her boyfriend Kris. This is where we see breathtaking pictures from a trip or a nature hike from our son Fernando with his fiancé Jaxon. This is where we see wonderful creativity come to life in a new clothing fashion design of our son Rodrigo. This is where we get to learn about important events in their lives with their loved ones, or with those soon to be their loved ones. This is where despite the distance, we get to do our virtual family "show and tell" about what we are proud of, what we are working on, and the plans that we have for the day, the "high-and low" of their day, their plans for the weekend, and more. This is where we get the daily question from Mamá to reflect on and get to read her pearls of wisdom on thoughts related to gratitude and abundance. This is where we all get famous quotes from me, many borrowed from other authors and a few penned down by me, to inspire our day ahead. This is where we all share the songs that we are listening to, and the ones we'd like to dance to, the TikTok videos of Fernando, and sometimes including Andrea and Rodrigo dancing as well.

And this is where we get excited about setting dates for the next time we will reunite, be it traveling to where they are, or traveling together elsewhere. No matter what we talk about, at the end of every conversation, when we sign off, we all contribute to continue adding to our 1 million "love you" and counting...

Key Takeaways:

Frequent and lively communication is what feeds and keeps a family together. No matter how busy we all might be, there is always time to share what is happening in our day and to check-in with each other.

A family chat is like a family get together. While the typing happens asynchronously most of the time, it synchronizes every member of the family on what really matters for all.

Song:

"Count on Me" – Bruno Mars

524 ever!

"The most wonderful places to be in the world
are in someone's thoughts, in someone's prayers
and in someone's heart." – Unknown

In my career as Human Resources leader, I have seen many things that can help bring people together, to coalesce behind a purpose and to work side-by-side towards achieving outstanding results, transforming the status-quo, and devoting their best efforts to a worthy cause. One of the most effective yet simple interventions is to find a "rallying cry" for their team, for their organization.

A rallying cry is a short phrase or slogan that instantly represents what people hold most dear about their particular organization. It is the ideological glue that brings them together, no matter how different they are, and it is the catalyst that requires no further explanation; once you hear it, you get it and get going towards it.

Notable examples of most memorable rallying cries for some companies are: "Just Do It!" (Nike), "Think Different" (Apple), "Never Settle" (One Plus), "Impossible Nothing" (Adidas), "Touching lives, improving life" (P&G). When you are part of those companies, you hear those words and you feel inspired, you feel the connection with who you are, you feel that you belong, and you find meaning in what you do every day.

I believe the same happens with families and at any stage of life. Like any other team of people, a rallying cry can unite and bring them altogether and make their bonds stronger. That has been the case for our family. In 2017, on a trip to California to visit our kids, we decided to go on a family hike in Los Angeles. Our son

Fernando, an avid hiker, took us to the "Wisdom Tree" trail, one of the most popular in the area, right in the middle of Hollywood.

The Wisdom Tree is the only tree that survived the 2007 Barham fire, it stands tall at the top of Cahuenga Peak, which is the highest peak at the end of Griffith Park and has become an inspiration hike for so many people. When we arrived at the top, we saw the tree and behind it a beautiful view of the entire city. After the customary pictures near the tree, climbing the tree (which is perfectly allowed), with my wife hugging the tree, and of the city views, we noticed an area close to the tree, with many rocks on the floor that had handwritten paper notes below each rock. Our son Fernando told us that it has become sort of a natural "shrine" where anyone can leave a handwritten note, expressing gratitude, sending love out to the universe, and sharing best wishes for anyone else that would do the hike and would become curious seeing the messages and might feel compelled to do the same.

That was our case indeed, we felt inspired as a family to leave our message of gratitude and love to each other. My wife found a blank piece of paper and with a blue pen wrote down: "Thanks God for all your blessings. Family First Forever. 5-2-gether", meaning the 5 family members (my wife, our three kids and myself) were together. We all held in a family hug and as we were talking about it, our son Fernando said: "5-2-gether-4ever", and our family rallying cry was born as: 524ever!

And with this rallying cry we keep moving forward as a family into the future. It is a reminder that our family has grown very strong roots, with all our traditions, rituals and experiences that we acquired moving around and abroad multiple times. It is a fire within that continues to invite each one of us to expand our wings into the world, to meet new and different people, to try new things, to leave our comfort zone, to learn about others, to help and give as much as we possibly can, and experience everything the world and this beautiful life has to offer. It is an unstoppable force that binds us together, through distance and time, with the bonds that we have created, forged in our intentional desire to be present in our lives. To have magnificent birthdays, anniversaries, holidays, and celebrations with eloquent toasts. To collect experiences and treasured heart shaped rocks from everywhere. To welcome new family members, to live and enjoy all the special moments together, to savor those small first steps as much as those giant milestones. To laugh uncontrollably, to dance until we cannot stand, to cry and openly express our emotions. To travel near and far, to just lay down on the grass watching the sky, the clouds, the stars, or to get going, to move, to hike to the top of a mountain or down to rivers and beaches to witness majestic sunsets and explore the world yet to discover.

**Whatever this life brings,
we choose to be intentional,
and we are 524ever!**

Song:

"Nothing's Gonna Stop Us Now" – Starship

Family Roots, Wings and Bonds Checklist

This is a selection of our "family greatest hits" that you can consider to be more intentional with your family:

1. Develop your personal PVP statement
   (Purpose, Values, Principles)

2. Define your personal Goals for each of the key roles
   in your life.

3. Write down and exchange your Vows for your
   relationship with your spouse/significant other.

4. Develop your Family Purpose, Goals, Principles.
   Do your Vision Boards on New Years Day.

5. Daily Habits: Reading with kids, Bedtime Conversations,
   Daily Hugs and Kisses.

6. Dedicated One-to-One time between each parent with
   each kid: Do something they love as often as possible.

7. Make a list of your Family Rituals and Traditions
   (Christmas, holidays, unique inherited rituals,
   home country culture) and share it with your family.

8. Plan your own version of "The Gift You Really Need"
   for your next holiday gathering.

(continued)

9. Travel together, involving kids in the planning, getting them excited, assigning them responsibilities over parts of the trip.

10. Foster Ownership and Accountability - Enable them to Do Chores as early as possible, give them responsibilities and rewards. Teach your kids the basics of personal Financial Responsibility.

11. Dance together! and make every celebration special and memorable. Lead a Toast and invite others to join and do the same.

12. Do Community Service and Volunteering as a family, do it as often as possible.

13. Have a Book Club with your kids at any stage of life.

14. Get to know their Friends at any stage.

15. Talk about their Relationships and love interests frequently.

**To learn more about our programs
for personal growth, you can visit our website:**

www.524ever.com

Songs by Themes

Family Love Language
"Home" – Michael Bubble
"Lost" – Michael Bubble
"Have It All" – Jason Mraz
"Lucky" – Jason Mraz, Colby Caillat
"I Hope You Dance" – Lee Ann Womack
"Sin Miedo" – Rosana
"Color Esperanza" – Diego Torres
"I Could Not Ask for More" – Edwin McCain
"Back Home" – Andy Grammer

Family Roots
"Hasta la Raiz" – Natalia Lafourcade

Discovering Your Purpose, Values, Principles
"Man in the Mirror" – Michael Jackson
"Hacia Lo Alto" – Eduardo Ortiz

Self-Motivation
"This Is My Time" – Amy Stroup
"Where My Heart Will Take Me" – Diane Warren, Russell Watson

Inspiration for Couples' Vows
"I Do" – Colbie Caillat
"Would You Go with Me" – Josh Turner
"You Decorated My Life" – Kenny Rogers
"I Want Crazy" – Hunter Hays
"Little Things" – One Direction
"Para Amarnos Más" – Mijares
"Todo Cambió" – Camila
"Para Siempre" – Kany Garcia
"A Fuego Lento" – Rosana
"Algo Contigo" – Rita Payes, Elisabeth Roma

New Baby's Arrival
"Duerme" – Jack Rabbit
"You'll Be in My Heart" – Phil Collins
"Bubbly" – Colby Caillat
"God Must Have Spent a Little More Time on You" – NSYNC

Family Purpose and Goals
"A Million Dreams" – Lucy Thomas

Enjoy the Simple Things in Life
"The Best Day (Taylor's Version)" – Taylor Swift
"Days Like This" – Busby Marou

Driving with the Family
"El Taqui Taqui – Original Mix" – Ilegales
"Ultimate" – Lindsay Lohan
"Iko, Iko (My Bestie)" – Justin Wellington, Small Jam
"Viva la Vida" – Coldplay

Happy Birthday and "Las Mañanitas"
"Las Mañanitas" – Mariachi Vargas de Tecalitlán
"Las Mañanitas" – Tatiana
"Happy Birthday To You" – Happy Occasion Singers
"Parabéns pra Você" – SaraoMusic

Celebrating Life
"What a Wonderful World" – Louis Armstrong

Turning a House into a Home
"Home" – Phillip Phillips
"Que No Falte Hogar" – Eduardo Ortiz Tirado, Cantantes Inhumyc

Playing with Your Kids
"You've Got a Friend in Me" – Randy Newman
"With Arms Wide Open" - Creed

Cafecitos (Coffee Dates) with Mom
"I'll Be Here" – Colbie Caillat, Sherryl Crow

Celebrating Mexican Heritage
"Cielito Lindo" – Pablo Montero
"Mexico Lindo y Querido – En Vivo" – Alejandro Fernández
"Huapango Moncayo (1941)" – Alondra de la Parra, Philarmonic Orchestra of the Americas

Promises Made – Promises Kept
"One Call Away" – Charlie Puth
"Stand by Me" – Ben E. King

"Honey Do List" / "Daddy Do List"
"I'll Be There" – Mariah Carey
"Godspeed (Sweet Dreams)" – The Chicks

Solving Conflicts Without Damaging Relationships
"Still into You" – Paramore
"You're Still the One" – Shania Twain

My Space, Our Space
"Our House" - Madness

Spirituality in Action, Volunteering, Community Service
"Heal the World" – Michael Jackson
"Rise Up" – Andra Day
"Look For The Good" – Jason Mraz
"Shine Your Light" – Master KG, David Guetta, Akon

Expressing Family Love –
"1 Million Kisses and I Love You and Counting"
"I Love You" - Barney

The Christmas Gift You Need
"All I Want for Christmas Is You" – Mariah Carey
"Esta Navidad" - Pandora

Keep Your Extended Family Close
"Father and Son" – Yusuf / Cat Stevens

Friends for Life
"Sweet Arizona" – East Love
"Festa" – Ivete Sangalo
"Danza Kuduro" – Don Omar, Lucenzo
"La Vida Es un Carnaval" – Celia Cruz

Family Wings
"Wind Beneath My Wings" – Bette Midler

Family Rocks
"Heirlooms" – Amy Grant

Catch Them When They Fall and When They Succeed
"The Last One" – Maisie Peters

Do Your Best and Make Good Choices
"Up, Up, Up" – Rose Falcon

Reading with Mom
"Greatest Love of All" – Whitney Houston

Doing Chores, Developing Ownership and Accountability
"Takin' Care of Business" – Bachman-Turner Overdrive

Mamá's Polvitos Mágicos (Mom's Magic Dust)
"Do You Believe in Magic?" - Aly & AJ
"Every Little Thing She Does Is Magic" – The Police
"You Can Do Magic" - America

Becoming Yourself When Everything Around You Changes
"Unwritten" – Natasha Bedingfield
"Hold On" – Wilson Phillips

Social Interactions, Finding Their Own Voice
"Brave" – Sara Bareiles

Dance Like Everyone Is Watching!

"La Ventanita" - Garibaldi
"Te Contarán" – Juan Luis Guerra
"Yo No Sé Mañana" – Luis Enrique
"Can't Stop This Feeling" – Justin Timberlake
"Dancing with Myself" – Billy Idol
"Footloose" – Kenny Loggins
"Arerê – Ao Vivo" – Banda Eva

College Essays – A Jewel of Self-Discovery

"This Is Me" – Keala Settle
"Don't Stop Me Now" – Queen
"Best Day of My Life" – American Authors

FOMO, YOLO, JOMO – Focus on What Really Matters

"I Lived" – One Republic
"Vienna" – Billy Joel
"Solo Se Vive una Vez" - Azucar Moreno

Finding a Prince/Princess – and Slaying a Few Dragons Along the Way

"Zanesville, Ohio" – Andy Leon
"Breadcrumbs" – Andy Leon
"The Stack" – Jack Rabbit
"This Again" – Jack Rabbit
"End the Daydream (from **Fitting In** Original Movie)" – Jack Rabbit
"Can't Help Falling in Love" – Elvis Presley
"Si Tú la Quieres" – David Bisbal
"Por el Resto de Tu Vida" – Christian Nodal, TINI
"Making Love Out of Nothing at All" – Air Supply

From Ally to All-In

"Malibu" – Miley Cyrus

Do What You Love – Love What You Do

"Good Job" – Alicia Keys

Family Bonds
"Better Together" – Jack Johnson

Going Away, Not Moving Out
"My Wish" – Rascal Flatts
"Never Grow Up" – Taylor Swift

Oh! the Places We Go...
"Oh, the Places You'll Go" – Anthem Lights
"Life is a Highway" – Rascal Flats
"Perderme Contigo" – Bacilos

Our New Roots, in a New Place, Together
"We've Only Just Begun" – The Carpenters

"Full Nesting" Filled with Love
"Three Little Birds" – Bob Marley & The Wailers
"Conselho" – Nanda Garcia

Getting to Know Their Friends at Every Stage
"I'll Be There for You" – The Rembrandts

Filling the Gaps
"Keep Your Head Up" – Andy Grammer
"Bad Day" – Daniel Powter

FAM JAM
"Count on Me" – Bruno Mars

524 ever!
"Nothing's Gonna Stop Us Now" – Starship

Spotify Playlist:
Roots, Wings and Bonds

about VITALITY

VITALITY is a circle of friends welcoming all, awakening each other, and reminding each other that we are Whole. Our affordable self-care programs invite everyone to move, to breathe, to rest, to contemplate, to grow...wherever each person begins their self-care journey, wherever and however they want to become.

It's the power of a circle!

We invite you to explore with us through our

donation-based classes...in person & via Zoom
affordable trainings
individual sessions
volunteer opportunities

vitalitycincinnati.org

VITALITY

buzz, bliss + books

publishing books from VITALITY's circle of friends
inspiring love, creativity, + possibility

vitalitybuzz.org

www.ingramcontent.com/pod-product-compliance
Lightning Source LLC
Chambersburg PA
CBHW070959120626
46546CB00004B/1697